College Survival Guide

Portable Edition

REAL STUDENTS. REAL EXPERIENCES. REAL ADVICE.

Ken Paulsen

WILEY

Wiley Publishing, Inc.

Dedicated to my parents, Harold and Gloria Paulsen.

Published by Wiley, Hoboken, NJ
Published simultaneously in Canada

For general information on our other products and services or to obtain technical support please contact our Customer Care Department within the U.S. at 800-762-2974, outside the U.S. at 317-572-3993 or fax 317-572-4002.

Wiley also publishes its books in a variety of electronic formats. Some content that appears in print may not be available in electronic books.

ISBN-10: 0-470-05646-0
ISBN-13: 978-0-470-05646-2

Manufactured in the United States of America

10 9 8 7 6 5 4 3 2 1

Book design by LeAndra Hosier

Cover design by José Almaguer

Page creation by Wiley Publishing, Inc. Composition Services

Table of Contents

Introduction

High school students spend endless hours choosing a college. They use guides to contrast schools. They surf the Internet, evaluating Web sites and getting a feel for each college's personality. They e-mail current undergraduates to get firsthand accounts from campus. And they may travel to five or more schools, checking out the scene, meeting faculty, and inspecting the dorms.

They take their time, because they want to get it right.

But choosing a school is only the first big decision of college life. Dozens more follow: How will I deal with alcohol issues? How can I get help if I have some sort of serious problem, from homesickness to depression? What adjustments should I consider after receiving my grades? Should I accept that great-sounding credit-card offer?

The process for making these critical decisions is far less exhaustive than choosing a college. A sophomore may decide in a snap whether to drink another beer at a party—a choice fraught with life-altering consequences. A freshman caught in a cash crunch may take a $500 cash advance on a credit card, kick-starting a debt cycle that might persist for a decade. On the positive side, a depressed student who knows that his resident adviser can point him towards help may take that vital first step. A student who vows to improve on a 2.8 first-semester grade-point average—aiming instead for a 3.5—will position herself well for law school; she won't have to "wake up" in her junior or senior year and frantically try to boost her grades.

Although college students may draw on the guidance they have received from Mom, Dad, and their teachers, they tend to make these decisions on their own. They relish the challenge of charting their own course, even if the path is bumpy. In less heady terms, they will not let anyone tell them what to drink, when to study, or how to manage their personal crises.

They will, however, note how others have managed in the same situations. And they may very well apply those experiences to their own lives.

That's where *College Survival Guide* comes in. It comprises the insights and experiences of more than 150 students at colleges and universities of all kinds, from every corner of the United States. Its premise is that, after spending months or years deciding where to attend college, students should stop and give serious thought before making the big decisions they'll face in college.

The central theme of *College Survival Guide* is that there is immense value in carefully considering the consequences of one's actions, for better or worse. This quickly emerged from students' explanations of how they handled important choices, ranging from dining hall selections to study habits to roommate conflicts.

Moderation serves as a secondary theme, applicable to the use of credit cards and alcohol, the time spent with boyfriends and girlfriends, and even sleep. "Not too much, and not too little" was the subtext of many students' approaches to college life.

These concepts are not presented out of context. Instead, they manifest themselves through the real experiences of college students who recognize the self-discovery that takes place at this unique time of their lives. Through poignant anecdotes, students candidly explain their choices and the consequences.

One student tells how she and her friends chose to break down a door to extract their dazed, drunken friend from a rendezvous with a guy she hardly knew—a situation where nothing good would have happened if they did not act. Another student details how she and three fellow freshmen decided to act on their dreams by starting their own student leadership group—one that's now spreading to other universities. And many students, through different experiences, relate how they languished in a "comfort zone," and only began getting the most out of college life when they elected to break out of that zone.

While I conducted some on-campus interviews for *College Survival Guide,* I did most by e-mail—a new approach for me, but one that proved to yield fruitful results. At first, I was concerned that the students would be too calculating in their e-mail responses, but the opposite proved to be true. With time to explain their mistakes and their smart moves in context, they opened up, clearly mindful of this information's value to new students. I was heartened that so many of the students expressed their appreciation for this book's concept—saying they wished they had read something like this when they began college.

I chose the students from a broad range of backgrounds and academic experiences, but admittedly slanted my selection towards those involved in leadership positions, whether through student government, resident adviser work, or involvement in campus activities.

I am grateful to the students who took the time to speak and correspond with me. Despite their own hectic schedules and commitments, they found the time to contribute. Their thoughtful comments and expressions of enthusiasm provided a spark that made writing this book a pleasure and an honor.

My deepest thanks are reserved for my wife, Sandy, and our children, Kathryn and Conor. They provide all the love, support, and inspiration I could ever ask for.

—Kenneth J. Paulsen

1

Before Arriving on Campus

> *Think of it as MTV's* The Real World *without cameras. You need to adjust to other people, but still maintain a strong sense of who you are.*
>
> —Vinda Rao, Tufts University, Class of 2006

Even if you've never been camping before, you probably know the importance of planning for a trip into the deep woods. You'd follow some basic rules: Take only what you need, so you don't have to carry around extra stuff. Pack enough food and water. Do not, under any circumstances, forget mosquito repellent. Expect to have fun and learn something new, but don't expect especially private or luxurious accommodations.

Well, mosquitos aren't a big problem on most college campuses. And relax—food and water are plentiful. But what you take to school—from your mindset to your mittens—may have a lot to do with how smoothly the first semester goes. This chapter will explore some of the questions students face before they head to college for the first time.

What should I take with me—and what should I leave home?

Filled with anticipation for her first semester at New York University, Stephanie Whited (Class of 2005) packed everything she could possibly need, especially clothes. Seven suitcases contained just about her entire wardrobe. "I couldn't bear to think that I might want to wear something I had left at home," she remembers.

But when she arrived on campus, Stephanie ended up mostly wearing the same favorites she wore at home in Memphis, Tennessee.

"While I was packing for school and going through my closet at home, I made the mistake of thinking that I might wear things I hadn't worn in at least a year," says Stephanie. "But that never happened. A couple of cool T-shirts, one favorite necklace, two pairs of pants, and comfortable sneakers were all I really needed. A lot of the clothes I never wore just filled up space in my dresser and closet and made unnecessary messes when I would have to dig through them to find what I needed."

All this explains her advice, borne out of experience, when it comes to packing for college: "Bring less clothes." Danielle Kittredge followed the "less is best" game plan when she prepared for her first year at the University of Pittsburgh. Everything went fine . . . until it started to get chilly, as it always does in western Pennsylvania. "I only brought stuff for the fall," she says, and T-shirts didn't exactly keep her toasty after sunset, or in air-conditioned classrooms. Home for Danielle, however, was only about an hour away, in Carmichaels, Pennsylvania, so her folks brought sweaters and sweatshirts early in the semester, leaving one less frostbitten freshman on campus. Motto: Bring enough but not too much.

Before you receive your dorm-room key, you'll have to decide, like Danielle and Stephanie, what to take with you to campus. The choice is appropriate to start this book, because it epitomizes the book's theme: Consider your decisions carefully, because you have to live with the results of them.

Stephanie and Danielle turned out just fine. Their packing missteps didn't cast a cloud over their freshman year. They probably won't ever gather their grandchildren in a circle by the fireplace and relate, "Did I ever tell you about the time I didn't pack properly for college?"

But both wish they did things differently, because it would have given them one less thing to be concerned about during one of the most hectic, thrilling times of their lives.

Deciding what to take sounds easy, doesn't it? Well, it's easy to remember most of the things you need. But it's also easy to take much more than you need. If you do take more than you need, you might have a hard time sleeping—because you'll barely have room to stand in your cramped room. And it's easy to forget some small items that can make your life easier, as anyone who's tried to open a can of soup with a pocketknife can tell you.

Of course, the answer lies somewhere in the middle. You know the middle, right? It's that big place somewhere between "going overboard" and "woefully unprepared."

For starters, if you didn't wear it, read it, watch it, listen to it, or use it at home, you probably won't do so at school. The only exceptions are items you absolutely need at school that you may not need at home, such as cold-weather gear.

Students may lean toward underpacking more than overpacking because they know if they forget something, they can still arrange to get it 99 percent of the time, whether they end up buying it or having it shipped from home.

But students warn against overpacking. They know that overpacking causes headaches that can't easily be fixed. Before you pack sweaters or jeans you never wore last winter, or before you take those CDs you've already burned to your computer, ask yourself: Do I really need them?

"I think everyone overpacks for college," says Michael Minvielle (American University, Class of 2005). He remembers arriving from his hometown of New Orleans for his first year in Washington, D.C. Among his many unnecessary possessions were games such as checkers, chess, and Monopoly. "You get to college, and find out there's no space for it."

No time, either.

Erica Johnson took lots of videos with her when she started her studies at the University of Delaware in the fall of 2003: "I didn't watch any of them." She was too busy enjoying college life to sit still for movies.

Michael says he also brought many books from home, figuring he'd read them in his free time. He didn't even open them up. "If I did read, it was for homework."

When you overpack, you can't escape it; besides being a constant reminder of your inefficiency, the unused stuff takes up precious space—in your drawers, in your closet, or on your desk. At the end of the year, you either have to lug that stuff back home or store it. Many students just throw it out, accounting for all the overflowing dumpsters parked outside of residence halls every May.

"You've got to find a way to box it, or ship it—or store it or throw it out," Michael Minvielle says. "It's no fun."

What to Leave Behind	
Items you don't regularly use now, and have no reason to begin using at school	It's unlikely you'll start using them now.
Valuable jewelry	These items can easily be lost or stolen, and they are never necessary on campus.

Anything delicate	If you take such items, you risk hearing a fellow freshman utter the immortal words, "Dude, I am SO sorry!"
Big users of electricity such as microwaves, air conditioners, or hot plates	Unless your college explicitly permits them, they'll be taken away; you may be breaking the rules, and you'll still have to lug them home next spring.
Candles	Possession of these is a big violation at most colleges—except for approved religious reasons—because they pose a fire hazard, especially when used by students who've been drinking.
Pets	Okay, maybe a goldfish.

What to Take

Clothes

- ❑ Plenty of the kinds of clothes you wear every day
- ❑ Baseball hats
- ❑ At least one semiformal outfit
- ❑ Casual shoes, sneakers, dress shoes
- ❑ At least 10 days' worth of underwear
- ❑ Socks (good and sport), also hosiery
- ❑ Sleepwear
- ❑ Clothing appropriate for the weather you'll encounter while you're on campus, including, if necessary, a heavy coat or jacket, mittens/gloves, hat, earmuffs, scarf, and boots
- ❑ No matter how warm your campus is: a sweater/sweatshirt, windbreaker, and a pair of jeans and/or sweatpants for the cooler days

- ❑ No matter how cold your campus is: T-shirts and several pairs of shorts—your dorm might be maintained at an uncomfortably warm temperature
- ❑ Hangers
- ❑ Rain gear
- ❑ Swimming attire
- ❑ Flip-flops and a bathrobe for the shower in your shared bathroom
- ❑ Gym attire

Food and Food-Related Items

- ❑ Snacks that won't spoil, including peanut butter, crackers, pretzels/chips, cookies, and granola bars
- ❑ Case of bottled water; powdered drink mix
- ❑ Macaroni and cheese mix, noodle-soup packets, breakfast cereal
- ❑ For the fridge: fruit, dairy products, soda, jelly, cheese (hold off on buying perishibles until you're close to campus)
- ❑ Microwave, if permitted; check if your dorm already has one in a common area
- ❑ Paper plates, cups, and plastic utensils; two sets of "real" utensils, plus a bowl and plate
- ❑ Tea, coffee, sugar, and coffeemaker, if permitted

Essentials

- ❑ Personal hygiene supplies and a bucket in which to carry shower supplies
- ❑ Comforter, pillow, two pillowcases, four sheets
- ❑ Towels, including one beach towel if you think you'll need it, and washcloths
- ❑ Backpack
- ❑ Pens and pencils
- ❑ Alarm clock-radio
- ❑ Telephone with answering machine, or cellphone with voicemail

- ❑ Rolls of quarters for laundry
- ❑ Laundry detergent, bleach, stain remover; basket or duffel bag for laundry
- ❑ Iron
- ❑ Can opener, pots and pans, and plastic water pitcher
- ❑ Umbrella
- ❑ Fan
- ❑ Duct tape
- ❑ Power strip/surge protector

Touches of Home

- ❑ Posters (find out how your school prefers these items to be mounted)
- ❑ Photos
- ❑ High school yearbook
- ❑ Decorations/holiday lights, if permitted

Laptop, desktop, or neither?

Expect to use a computer every day you're on campus—whether to check out a professor's online postings, to surf the Web, or to e-mail friends and family, just to name a few frequent uses. The good news is that if you don't have a computer, and don't plan to get one, you'll do fine. But having one is a convenience that's worth paying for. The College Board reports that 2004–2005 college tuition (not counting room and board) averages more than $20,000 a year at private schools and more than $5,000 a year at public colleges. With those prices, an investment of less than $500 for a desktop computer or $800 for a laptop is a no-brainer. You'll be grateful every time you don't have to wait at a campus computer cluster or pester a friend to borrow her computer. It'll be yours, and you'll be free to use it whenever you want and (if you have a laptop) wherever you want.

"Your laptop becomes the most valuable item you own," says Anisa Mohanty (University of North Carolina at Chapel Hill, Class of 2007). "If I am in my dorm room, I am usually using my laptop

Considering a Laptop?

- ✓ Entry-level laptops cost less than $800.
- ✓ They're easy to take to class or the library. But they still weigh 3 to 7 pounds, and many students prefer to leave them in their dorm rooms.
- ✓ Their smaller keyboards and displays may make them more difficult to work on for long-term projects.
- ✓ They can be used to access the Internet from any point on campus through wireless fidelity (or wi-fi) networks at the increasing number of colleges that offer them.
- ✓ They are popular targets for thieves. Don't leave yours out of your sight in the library, and don't leave your dorm-room door open with the laptop in plain view.

for research, writing papers or essays, or simply for entertainment. It's also great to be able to take your laptop to your lecture classes to take notes, rather than writing pages upon pages of tedious notes."

That's not to say that the cost of a computer is pocket change, but rather that it's one purchase that justifies getting an additional loan or utilizing a monthly payment plan. A high-quality computer will represent a miniscule percentage of your overall college costs,

Considering a Desktop?

- ✓ Entry-level desktops cost less than $500.
- ✓ They can be clunky and difficult to move, and will take up desk space in your room.
- ✓ They are more likely to come with bigger screens than laptops, making them a better choice for movie-watching or working on certain kinds of projects.

and it will make your time in school much more productive. If you take a computer, you'll also need a printer and paper.

Chris Deal (Iowa State University, Class of 2007) says his laptop has been indispensable. "The biggest advantage of laptops is their ease of transportation," he says. "Whenever I went home or had to go somewhere to work on a project, it was a breeze to pack up my laptop and go."

Should I have a car on campus?

If you're fortunate enough to have a choice in this matter, it's tempting to say "yes." But having a car on campus can potentially be more hassle than it's worth.

Before you decide to take one with you to school, ask yourself: Why do I want a car? You probably want your car for the same reasons you want it at home—you'll have the freedom to go anywhere you want, whenever you want. It's a natural extension of the other freedoms you'll have while you're at school.

"I had my car on campus and I was really glad I did," says Elizabeth Flynn (University of Tennessee, Knoxville, Class of 2004). "It was just convenient to be able to go home when I wanted and not have to depend on someone else for a ride."

But students say the price of that freedom can be high:

- ✓ High parking fees—from $100 to $300 per year—are the rule at many colleges. On urban campuses, parking may be severely restricted.
- ✓ Very few parking options may exist on the streets around campus, eliminating the convenience of driving from one part of campus to another.
- ✓ Campus and city parking regulations are enforced with vigor—and steep fines—on and near most colleges. At Texas State University–San Marcos, for example, the cars of "chronic offenders" are impounded and the students face $150 fines, according to the university's Web site.
- ✓ Those with cars are frequently asked for rides from other students. At first, it's a nice way to make friends and to see the town. After a while, you might be tempted to paint your car yellow and install a meter.

The real issue is: Do you *need* a car? The nature of residential college campuses is that a car is not necessary, unless you have special needs. Everything's on campus, from your classes to the gym to your dorm. You'll do plenty of walking, no doubt, but it's not practical to expect to drive from one campus destination to another.

Elizabeth agreed that sometimes there's a down side to having your own car on campus. "Parking is expensive and a hassle—a year-long parking pass was about $245 at UT," she says. Another student at an urban university told of spotting people driving around for 45 minutes looking for a parking space.

Still, despite the hassle, a car will come in handy if your campus can accommodate it. Whether you take road trips, drive home, or explore the city, the convenience of door-to-door service is the upside to the hassle.

Many schools, in both urban and rural settings, have good public-transportation options. "Iowa State has a deal with [the city of] Ames where the 'CyRide' bus system is available free to all ISU students," said student Chris Deal. They can take the buses "not only around campus but also to all the major attractions in Ames. I still have a car with me, but I rarely use it."

And while a bus may not be as convenient as a car, the price is usually right, and there's no need to look for a parking space.

How will I "fit in" on campus?

Before freshman year begins, you might spend hours wondering what campus life will be like, how you'll interact with others, and how you'll fit in.

Fitting in, in the broadest sense, really just means being part of your college's community—it doesn't mean you're conforming to any prescribed behavior pattern. The good news, students say, is that the only key to fitting in, as we define it here, is being yourself.

In other words, the only approach rejected on campus is phoniness.

"Don't sacrifice who you are as an individual in order to fit in—that was middle-school stuff," says David Doerkin (University of California, Berkeley, Class of 2004).

David recalls two experiences where he had to choose between following the crowd and asserting his individuality—and both times he took the latter approach. Unlike most dorm floors with freshmen, David's floor was quiet. Students preferred to work at their computers with their doors closed, and socializing was minimal.

"I felt pretty alienated from the rest of the people on my floor," he says. "I wanted to go out and meet people, and the majority of my floormates were complete shut-ins with little inclination to go to parties. So I decided to go out on my own to meet people, and by a couple of weeks later, I had met some people with whom I'm still friends today. It just took some personal initiative and exploration, not falling into the patterns already adopted by other people."

Later in his college career, David happened across another issue that can divide campuses and groups of friends—the Greek system. Several of his friends wanted to join a fraternity. David had no interest.

"Instead of just going along with what my friends wanted to do, I spent some time exploring other options and found the co-op housing system, in which I have lived for the past three years," says David, referring to a group housing system at Berkeley in which students share responsibilities such as management, cooking, and maintenance. "I made many friends living in the co-ops without sacrificing what I wanted socially."

> *"I have met most of my best friends by doing what I love to do and being myself. College is the best time to get involved with new activities and meet tons of new people."*
>
> —Lindsay Baran, University of Illinois at Urbana-Champaign, Class of 2005

Another key to fitting in—being part of your campus community—is working together with your fellow students. This can seem difficult, since you likely know very few of them. But college freshmen, despite all the talk of diversity, are bound by many similarities:

- ✓ They arrive on campus at roughly the same age.
- ✓ They excelled, to some degree, in high school, and must prove themselves again.
- ✓ They're experiencing their first taste of freedom.
- ✓ They've never lived with a stranger before.
- ✓ They know relatively little about their new living and academic environment.

As a result, basic courtesy—communication, cooperation, and respect—accomplishes more than any planned personality approach. As the following chapters will show, open communication, which includes listening as well as speaking, is a key to navigating the complexities of college life.

2

The First Few Days

> *The most common phrase I heard throughout the year was, 'This is so-and-so whom I met at Frosh-O.' I'd say it is the best way to get to know your friends and classmates.*
>
> —Bill Andrichik, University of Notre Dame, Class of 2006, speaking about freshman orientation

You're on your own. This fact may not hit you until your parents drive into the distance after helping you get settled. No one will comment on the hours you maintain, the clothes you wear, the company you keep, or your mounting list of chores. (Your R.A. might have something to say if you blast your stereo, but we'll get to that later.)

From now on, the decisions you make are yours. Don't want to do the laundry tonight—or this week? Let it pile up. Feel like sleeping until noon, even though you have class at 9:30 a.m.? Snooze away. Not interested in working more than one afternoon a week at your part-time job? No sweat—tell the boss that's all you can handle.

Of course, while you're free to make those decisions, it helps to think them through.

Doing laundry has never been fun—but the dreadful alternative is running out of clean underwear. Skipping class might seem logical when you've had a late night, but do it often and you might discover the logic behind a C or D grade in philosophy class. And if you choose to work the bare minimum at your campus job, you may not have much cash to spend during your free time.

This chapter explores some of the decisions you'll confront in the first days on campus, from attending orientation and dealing with fire alarms to setting up your room and interacting with your resident adviser. In many ways, the choices made at this point can help ensure that your college experience begins successfully.

Should I attend all these first-week gatherings?

Somewhere on the endless list of things to do as you get settled will be at least one—or two, or three—orientation or welcome events.

There might be a session for all members of your incoming class—a convocation where college officials greet you, charge you with great responsibilities, and remind you that you won't be gathered again in similar fashion until graduation day. A smaller get-together might take place just for freshmen in your degree program or "home college."

And you can certainly expect at least one gathering in your dorm, where you'll meet your R.A. (resident adviser or resident assistant) and floormates.

At many of these gatherings, especially those involving your residence hall, you'll likely engage in some form of "ice-breaker" activity—to get to know your peers. These events provide one of your first opportunities to try out your new freedoms—you can skip any or all of them, and no one will notice.

Should you? You won't know until you go, unfortunately. But students say the time is almost always well spent.

"As humdrum as an orientation sounds, it might be the most worthwhile activity you do your first semester at school," says Jon Hoggatt (Purdue University, Class of 2005). At Purdue, students attending orientation can check in a few days before most others arrive on campus, allowing extra time to explore new surroundings.

That extra time and the orientation activities are especially useful to those who don't want to look too much like freshmen once classes start. Orientation allowed Jon to start the semester with confidence: "Orientation is a great time to get familiar with

Perhaps the most telltale sign of a freshman is the bewildered look and the slow 360-degree turn in place while trying to figure out if O'Sullivan Hall is on the quad's north side or south side–and which way is north, anyway? With few options, the campus map comes out–the one that might as well state, in big, bold letters:

"CLUELESS FRESHMAN'S GUIDE TO CAMPUS"

Look on the bright side though: While you're struggling with the map, someone will likely spot you before long and take pity–and you might even make a new friend.

campus—so you don't get lost going to your classes the first week. And many will educate you on traditions at your new school . . . you definitely want to know how to sing your fight song at the first football game."

Lara Bennett (University of Scranton, Class of 2006) admits that orientation might seem like a clichéd activity that can be boring and a waste of time. But she knew it also might hold something positive for her.

She was right (about the positive part, that is). So she went.

And she was glad she did.

"All the 'stupid' activities they make you participate in really help you meet people and get to feel more comfortable in your new environment," she says. "Everyone is in the same boat that you are—always remember that."

The ice-breakers can fluster even the most outgoing freshmen. You might be asked to describe your road-test experience—a sure way to provide some insights into your personality. Or everyone in a group of 20 might be asked to take off a shoe, put it in a pile, retrieve another, then go around meeting everyone until they've met the rightful owner.

The activities are done to get you to drop your defenses and open up. Laughing at yourself may be the best way to do that—just about everyone has a laugh-out-loud funny story about a driving experience, right? And although you may be mortified while carrying around someone's sneaker for five . . . long . . . minutes, the others doing the same thing will feel the same way—so you can't help but smile at each other. As awkward as the ice-breakers can be, they can work magically. By putting students with so much common ground together, orientation helps forge bonds among them.

Jeff Bonnett (University of Pittsburgh, Class of 2004) remembers how easy it was to make friends during orientation. "They all got that scared look on their face: We need to make friends," he recalls of the shared freshman orientation experience.

While relaxing on the lawn near Pitt's towering Cathedral of Learning on a clear spring Sunday morning, Jeff and his buddy Dennis Curlett, also Class of 2004, reflected on their fun-filled first year. When the guys heard about some fellow freshmen hosting a party, they eagerly helped spread the word. They did a great job, as evidenced by the overflow crowd. And they ended up making lots of lasting friendships. They traced those friendships, at least in part, to their willingness to circulate and play ice-breakers like a version of MTV's "Singled Out." Says Dennis, looking back: "In your freshman year, you make 90 percent of your friends."

Bill Andrichik (University of Notre Dame, Class of 2007) says his freshman orientation was extensive but incredibly useful. "Ours lasted about four days and consisted of dozens of activities that were both dorm-wide and campus-wide," says Bill. "Since we have 27 unisex dorms, the majority of the activities were things such as dances and water fights with different girls' dorms. While the activities could get kind of corny at times, the most common phrase I heard throughout the year was, 'This is so-and-so whom I met at Frosh-O.' I'd say it is the best way to get to know your friends and classmates."

How should I set up my room?

Dictionaries define dormitory as "a place to sleep." They usually don't say much about studying, eating, listening to music, hanging out, or hosting parties—but all those things happen in dorms, too. Maybe that's why many colleges now call them residence halls, reflecting that students don't just sleep in those places—they live there.

Despite the small size and unimaginative layouts of most dorm rooms, there's room to set up yours in a way that suits your style and all that you do in your room. Resourcefulness and imagination are the key ingredients to personalizing your room.

Rooms are typically furnished with curtains or a shade, a closet, dresser, desk and chair, and sometimes a bookshelf that might or might not be bolted to the wall. Those standard-issue items won't show up in the pages of *Dorm Beautiful* magazine, but they are functional—they serve their purposes well.

Jacqueline Victor (University of Colorado at Boulder, Class of 2006) says a smart division of space helped her adapt to the "constrained box" feel of her dorm rooms. "For eight months out of each year, this area is the one place I can call my own," she says of her sophomore-year single room. "I find that creating a mini home makes my life so much better. For example, I organize a sleeping space with my bed, a study space using a lounging chair, a workspace for my computer, a kitchen space by my refrigerator, and a preparation space near my mirror and products." Each space may be tiny, but it's also distinct. A similar approach worked well her freshman year, she says, when she shared a double room. Each roommate had her own partitioned area, and they shared a common area.

Comfort has been the top priority of Lindsay Baran when setting up her rooms—it's an approach she suggests other students keep in mind. "You don't want it to be too cluttered or too empty," says Lindsay (University of Illinois at Urbana–Champaign, Class of 2005).

Lots of students straddle the line between comfort and clutter, though. For that reason, organizers of every possible kind—for papers, notes, pens, computer discs, clothes, and much more—are pitched to college students. It might be tempting to buy lots of them. They can be useful if you have a lot of stuff that's tough to keep track of, but it depends on how much stuff you actually have, and whether an organizer can really make your life easier. For example, you may not need a fancy CD holder if you can just as easily stack your CDs on the bookshelf. But if you have 10 pairs of shoes, it might be worth buying a shoe organizer for your closet. In short, you don't want your room cluttered with organizers.

Laurel Cooper (Duke University, Class of 2005) suggests setting up your room according to "however things fit"—there are no set rules—and then seeing if organizers are needed. "Don't buy space savers until you arrive," she says, "since you probably won't have a clue how your stuff and your roomie's stuff will fit together."

The single biggest factor in how a room is set up might be which roommate arrives first. That person's choices can set the tone for decisions and adjustments that follow.

One of the most popular ways to create more space in dorm rooms is to "loft" one's bed—to build a structure that holds the mattress several feet off the ground. By freeing up floor space, students can stack stuff under the bed, such as small shelves to hold books, clothes, food, or stereo equipment. Some students use the space for a futon or beanbag chair.

"I would recommend lofting both of your beds because it creates lots of space," says Kristina Ihlenfeldt (Clemson University, Class of 2003). She cautions, however, to plan before making a move: "We rearranged my roommate's furniture while she was gone one weekend," and although the roommate approved of the loft, she didn't appreciate the fact that her bed was inches away from an air vent. "She had to sleep with extra blankets every night until we moved things around again."

Lots of other students choose to bunk—stack their bed on top of their roommate's, or vice versa. It's an easy way to re-claim the space taken by one of the beds.

Before you make any changes to your room's layout, consider these suggestions:

✓ Check with upperclassmen for advice. They've seen it all, and they can tell you what works and what doesn't. For example, they might agree with your idea to loft your bed—but they might warn that you better have a place to store the frame, because the university doesn't offer storage. Knowing that stipulation can save you hours of trouble.

> Make sure the beds are truly "bunkable" before you bunk them, and that you exercise caution while using any bed that's a few feet off the ground. Four University of Buffalo students were hurt by either falling or jumping out of bunk beds in the fall of 2003, according to the *Buffalo News*. One student who went to bed woke up on the floor with a bloody lip, not knowing how he got there, while another got hurt when she leaped out of the top bunk when the phone rang—or she possibly dreamed it rang. The university suspected drinking was playing a role in the incidents, and began installing guard rails on the beds.

- ✓ Make sure your plan follows the rules. You won't be able to hide the fact that your bed is lofted five feet in the air. If it's prohibited, your R.A. will find out sooner than later, and reluctantly tell you to take it down.
- ✓ Be prepared to undo everything if either roommate doesn't like the modifications. For example, bunking might sound great, and it might create much more space in your room—but you might not realize until the lights go out that the squeaking springs on your roommate's mattress, just inches away from your ears, drive you completely bananas.

No matter how you arrange your room, you'll have to return it to its original state when you check out at the end of the school year. Schools can forward to you the labor charges for any rearranging you neglect to do. And before you secure anything to the walls at the beginning of the year, find out what your school recommends. Different schools may have different regulations about thumbtacks, pushpins, nails, adhesive putty, or tape, and may levy charges if you leave behind "scarred" walls.

While rearranging or decorating your room can make it more livable and comfortable, the biggest factor is going to be how well you and your roommate communicate and respect each other's needs. When roommates are in sync on these matters, one's bed and study areas seem a lot more comfortable. When roommates are out of sync, they'd still be miserable if they were living in a luxury suite at the Ritz-Carlton.

> *"The room situation basically depends on how much stuff you have and who you are rooming with."*
>
> —Bill Andrichik, University of Notre Dame, Class of 2007

Should I be concerned about fire safety?

Irene Fernando (University of Minnesota, Twin Cities, Class of 2007) remembers the night before a big test. With some noisy neighbors

Middle-of-the-night fire alarms are an unfortunate fact of life for many college students. They are often deliberately pulled by students as pranks. Such students don't realize they may face felony charges and prison time for their actions—and that false alarms encourage apathy among students: They might not leave their rooms during the next alarm because they figure it's not a real fire.

both above and next door to her room, it took her awhile to fall asleep, even though she went to bed at 2 a.m. She was dozing off close to 3 a.m.—only six hours before her class—when a loud beeping startled everyone in her dorm.

The fire alarm pealed throughout the hallways, impossible to ignore, even among the half-awake and sound asleep. "What the hell is blaring right now?" she remembers thinking as she checked her clock. As if on cue, a booming automated voice provided the answer: "This is not a drill. There is a fire. Please file to your appropriate exit." She was shocked.

"This can't be happening," she remembers thinking. "I have a test tomorrow." But the rule about fire alarms is that they rarely happen at convenient times. (Think about it, though: Is there ever a convenient time for a fire alarm?)

So she went outside, in the frigid, dark Minnesota night, with fellow residents of her dorm. "You go out in your pajamas after throwing on a robe and slipping your sandals on. Everyone is miserable. It's got to be 10 degrees outside."

Irene took a good attitude with her as she filed down the stairs and out the door, although at first she was angry. "Who wouldn't be? I was complaining and angry with the best of them, until I realized that I was doing no one any good at all." It turned out that there was a real fire in the dorm that night. Although no injuries or major damage resulted from the fire, the message was clear to the students: Get outside when you hear the alarm.

Although the majority of fire alarms turn out to be false alarms, fires do happen, as Irene's experience suggests. Information provided by the U.S. Fire Administration and the National Fire Prevention Association make it clear why fire safety should be on students' minds:

- ✓ More than 1,700 fires occur in dormitories and in Greek housing each year, an average of about five a day.
- ✓ Arson or suspected arson, cooking, and careless smoking are the leading causes of campus fires.
- ✓ Alcohol is a major factor in many campus fires that result in fatalities.
- ✓ Many students do not consider fire to be a serious risk or threat, so they don't respond to alarms.

A false alarm problem in dorms is not something colleges eagerly mention to bright-eyed high-school seniors making their campus visits, so it may be a surprise to freshmen when they first experience one. The ear-splitting roar of an alarm at 2, 3, or 4 a.m. is so common at some dorms that students are tempted to roll over and try to go back to bed. For safety reasons, R.A.s may be authorized to enter students' rooms during fire alarms; those they discover intentionally staying behind are subject to fines or disciplinary action.

Fire safety is also behind the rules that won't let you arrange your room a certain way, and bans against appliances that might overload circuits. For the same reasons, candles and incense are usually prohibited, and an increasing number of schools ban smoking outright in their dorms. Given the circumstances—dozens, or hundreds, of students in a relatively confined place—fire safety is a top concern of hall administrators.

How should I deal with my R.A.?

During your years in college, you may spend dozens of hours in class with some professors, and meet many authority figures, but it's possible that no person representing your school will get to know you more personally than your R.A.

R.A. stands for resident adviser or resident assistant, but the R.A.'s role is the same at colleges across the country: to help new students adjust to life on campus, to act as a resource for all that the college offers, and to foster a sense of community among students living on a floor.

While some students will no doubt look upon R.A.s as meddlesome substitute parents, it's better to think of them as older, wiser brothers and sisters. They're there to offer help and guidance—and to lay down the law if it's necessary. More often than not, you'll be glad they're around. Here are some of the many areas where R.A.s can help you:

- ✓ Questions about college life, procedures, or people
- ✓ How to effectively use your college's unique meal plan
- ✓ How to cope with homesickness
- ✓ Where to find buildings on campus, and the best ways to get to them
- ✓ How to deal with roommate problems
- ✓ Options for on- and off-campus activities
- ✓ How to get involved in clubs and groups
- ✓ Where to get help if you're sick or depressed

That last point is the most important. While R.A.s receive plenty of training, they don't pretend to be experts on every subject. One of their specialities is referring students to the right source for help if the situation is beyond their grasp. That's why you can go to your R.A. with any problem—at the very least, you'll get pointed in the right direction.

R.A.s are usually juniors or seniors, but sometimes sophomores are selected. Competition is intense for the positions because the compensation is so good—free room and board at most schools. That competition usually results in a group of mature, knowledgeable R.A.s in each dorm.

Perhaps the best thing to keep in mind about R.A.s, according to Michael Minvielle (American University, Class of 2005), is that they're students, too. In other words, they've been through what you're going through, and it's their job to make college life easier for you.

Michael was surprised when he first got to know his freshman-year R.A. "It was not what I was expecting," he says. "He wasn't an authority figure—he was very relaxed."

That doesn't mean the R.A. allowed the floor to become a zoo; rather he set the tone of common respect. The same approach that keeps peace among roommates works at the floor level as well.

His R.A. was also a solid source of information about the university. Michael knew that when he had a basic question, "The R.A.'s your No. 1 choice. He's not going to make you feel stupid."

David Doerkin (University of California, Berkeley, Class of 2004) recalled his freshman year with an inflexible R.A. who was not willing to give students a break on anything. David suggests getting to know your R.A., regardless of how much you think you'll depend on him or her. "Spend some time observing how the R.A. acts or reacts to any given problem," he says, and you'll be better equipped when you have a problem of your own.

Although R.A.s possess varying levels of tolerance for student transgressions, the best way to stay on good terms is to follow the rules—especially those that involve safety, alcohol and drugs, university property, and excessive noise. Keep your nose clean in those areas, and you should expect smooth sailing.

> *"A lot of freshmen think that an R.A. is the bad guy, someone who will get you in trouble. But I had a really cool R.A. once. Try to be friends with them if you can and don't be intimidated by them. They are there to help you should you need it."*
>
> —Elizabeth Flynn, University of Tennessee, Knoxville, Class of 2004

"R.A.s go through substantial training before move-in and are very willing to help with all matters," says Dave Munson (Class of 2005), an R.A. at the University of Chicago. "Respect the rules and your relationship with your R.A. will be excellent."

3

Roommates

"I don't think I had a whole lot in common with either one of my roommates, but we didn't let that stand in the way of a pleasant living situation."

Denelle Walker, Louisiana State University, Class of 2006

When students talk about getting along with roommates, one word repeatedly surfaces: *communication.* The willingness to talk before problems arise, and to confront the problems that inevitably do occur, are critical to successful roommate relationships. "Successful " by the way, doesn't have to mean that you become dear friends who can't ever go to the dining hall without the other, as many students point out. It means that you're both civil to each other and, most importantly, you're both able to use and enjoy your own living space by cooperating and being considerate.

How can I get along with a roommate I have nothing in common with?

"They send you a letter, and the roommate is really just a name and a number," recalls Josh Johnston (University of Nevada, Reno, Class of 2005). "You don't know how you'll get along."

That's how it goes for most college students, such as Josh—initial anxiety is followed by an experience that's usually positive, but only because both roommates work at it.

Don't be surprised if your roommate is nothing like what you expected—that goes for students who are rooming with their best friend from high school as well as those bunking with a foreign-exchange student. Living with someone is far different from going to class or hanging out with them.

Rooming with someone unlike you doesn't foreshadow a miserable experience, though—far from it. And students paired with their mirror image may despise each other by the end of September. You won't know how it will go until you've met your roommate, and you've both had opportunities to show how much you're willing to make it work.

Jennifer Maden (University of Tennessee, Knoxville, Class of 2004) found this out at the beginning of her freshman year: "I had a roommate who was the complete opposite from me," she relates. "I went through sorority rush and she hated Greeks. I wanted our room to be bright and cheerful, while she came to school with an all-black comforter. On the outside we were completely different."

It didn't matter.

"I soon realized that it didn't matter that we had nothing in common. We could still be roommates. In the beginning, I tried to find small things that we did have in common . . . those things I would talk to her about, and soon I learned that we had more similarities than I thought."

Jennifer and her roommate got along well because they respected each other's space. For example, it didn't take long for each to realize the approximate time the other went to bed each night. So if one came home later, she'd be quiet. It may not be easy to appreciate the courtesy shown by a considerate roommate, especially when you sleep right through her return home—until you consider how a different person might turn on lights or the TV, or make a phone call, upon returning to the room at 3 a.m.

"Living with someone different than you are can be a good thing," Jennifer says. "You will have different interests, different schedules, and different friends, which will keep you all from getting on each other's nerves and allow you to share new experiences with the other person."

Denelle Walker (Louisiana State University, Class of 2006) has had good roommate experiences during both her freshman and sophomore years. She did not know her first roommate beforehand, while she was acquainted with the second before they lived together. "A common misconception is that you have to be 'B.F.F.' (best friends forever) with your roommates—and that is not the case. There is no requirement to have deep late-night chats and be attached at the hip."

Denelle says it worked out fine that she wasn't too close with either roommate. She sees her dorm room as just a small part of her college experience—a place to sleep, study, and, of course, hang out in, but not to excess. Her goal has always been to meet people and get involved—something that can't be done in the dorm room. With each roommate spending relatively little time in the room, there weren't many opportunities for problems to arise—it made it easier for them to appreciate the time they had together to catch up on things. Denelle adds that if roommates make a strong connection, that's great, but her priority is to be cordial, civil, and respectful.

How can I tell my roommate about something that's annoying me?

You'd probably tell a good friend if she had a piece of lettuce stuck between her front teeth. Of course you would—you're a good friend. But would you tell her if you noticed a small scuff mark on the back of her new shoes? Probably not.

Students say that knowing when to speak up is important, but it's also vital to know when to keep quiet. These skills help them smooth over rough patches with roommates before they escalate into tense situations. Good roommates know that no matter how much alike they are, no matter how well they know each other, and no matter how nice they are to each other, there are times when something rubs one of them the wrong way.

It's tough to broach these issues with roommates, but it's necessary, because not doing so can lead to a bigger problem. The most important step, students say, is how you present the situation.

> *"Be direct but use a nonconfrontational tone. It is also important to establish guidelines in the beginning of the year. If an aspect of your roommate's personality annoys you in September, don't assume that it will magically disappear over winter break."*
>
> —Dave Munson, University of Chicago, Class of 2005

Using a light touch is most helpful. An overly serious, dramatic, or, worst of all, angry request won't get results. And a touch of humor can only improve your chances for success.

Vinda Rao (Tufts University, Class of 2006) has seen how humor can clear the air with an issue that drives a wedge between many roommates: sloppiness. A roommate who observes a mess, stumbles over it, and gets disgusted by it, without discussing it, might quickly move to not discussing anything with her roommate.

"I'm not the neatest person in the world, and my roommate, who luckily turned out to be a great friend, started off by saying, 'Vinda, could you please consider maybe possibly picking up those books on the floor?' I looked at her like she had three heads," she recalls. "Then she laughed and said, 'Dude, get your stuff off the floor before I trip over it and sue you.' Obviously she wasn't serious, but being friendly with me and making a joke about it won me over, and I cleaned the room within an hour."

Vinda's glad her roommate told her about the messiness issue. It wasn't much trouble to fix and it allowed them to continue getting along. All too often, it only takes one episode of poor communication to send an otherwise good relationship down the drain. "Don't dance around the issue," Vinda says. "If something's getting on your nerves, tell your roommate directly, and tell them as soon as you feel annoyed. Letting something fester usually results in a huge blowout."

J.C. Ratigan (Texas Christian University, Class of 2007) is familiar with the prevailing advice against bottling up one's feelings.

"But in my case that's exactly what I did," he remembers of his freshman year, "and I just got more and more annoyed."

He agrees that the delivery of the message is critical. If you're too casual with a request, the roommate may not take you seriously, he says. And coming on too strong is a total turn-off. He says it depends on the roommate—so look for signs that he's trying to accommodate your direct request, and if not, bring it up gently, but seriously, a second time.

> *"I once roomed with a girl who loved* Court TV. *She would come in from her 8 a.m. class and turn on the television every day. If I wasn't sleeping, I was studying—and I hate* Court TV. *One day, I finally told her that it drove me crazy. She had no idea. She thought I liked the show because I would stop studying and 'watch.' I was really just willing the TV to blow up. After that conversation, she watched* Court TV *with headphones, and we were both happier."*
>
> —Rebecca Wood, University of Memphis, Class of 2005

How can we share some common expenses?

If your roommate's a little loud late at night, you might learn to get used to the chatter. If she's sloppy, you might learn to look past the heaps of dirty laundry. If he has some friends you're not wild about, you might plan to visit the library while the buddies hang around.

But if your roommate won't pay his share of the phone bill, or eats three quarters of the food you've paid for, it's another matter. In college, being out $20 is no small deal. To make it up, you might have to work the better part of an afternoon stocking shelves, making lattes, or working the cash register. When roommates mismanage shared expenses, one of them pays for it with her own precious time.

Anisa Mohanty (University of North Carolina at Chapel Hill, Class of 2007) offers blunt advice on avoiding these food fights: "Don't eat more than your half!"

Students take different approaches to food expenses, but they all have the same goal—keeping it fair. Below are three typical strategies:

✓ **Each buys his own food and never touches the other's.** The good part about this is that it eliminates squabbles over money. The downside is that it's not the ideal living arrangement. You share a tiny space; you should be able to share some essentials, such as a can of soda or some cookies, without stepping on each other's toes.

✓ **Shop together, splitting the bill, and sharing the food.** This might be the best arrangement, because you'll both talk things out as you shop and adjust your purchases accordingly. If you put a six-pack of Dr Pepper in the shopping cart and your roommate says "That's my favorite!" you'll know to pick up another and split the cost. This arrangement forces you to discuss what you want and what you eat before a misunderstanding occurs.

✓ **Shop separately and share the food within reason.** This might be the most common choice, because it's not always easy to line up your schedules and shop together. And rather than heading to a supermarket every week or two, each of you might be more inclined to stop at a convenience store on campus when you need to. If one person buys food for both of you one week, be sure the other understands it's her turn to return the favor next time.

Kristina Ihlenfeldt (Clemson University, Class of 2003, favors the third option. "Figure out what you both use, and trade off buying it whenever it runs out," she says. "Make sure you use it equally so one person doesn't always end up using twice as much as the other."

> *"Inevitably you eat different things, or one roommate eats more than the other. So, it is best to buy your own food but share maybe small things like condiments, milk, or butter. With items like these, it makes more sense to share because of expiration dates or space, and you can just trade off buying the items, so each time you run out, another person goes to get the next bottle."*
>
> —Jennifer Maden, University of Tennessee, Knoxville, Class of 2004

One student, who's a member of American University's class of 2007, suggests planning purchases with your roommate. "One can buy some things; the other can buy other stuff. If schedules don't allow for shopping together, make a list together of common items and agree to split the bill. We did a lot of this and it worked out really well."

She took this approach with other items when she got in touch with her roommate weeks before they arrived on campus for freshman year. "We agreed that one of us would bring the TV, the other the fridge. That way we didn't end up with two of an expensive item."

Kristina Ihlenfeldt did the same thing at Clemson and it worked well for her and her roommate. By figuring things out before they arrived on campus, they avoided the need to buy big items that they'd have to share. They saved money, and it also made it easy to figure out who gets what at the end of the year. Each person went home with the items she took to school.

Depending on the school, some items you might expect to pay for may be covered by your room fees, such as Internet and telephone access. Of course, students living off campus will pay separately for those items.

When it comes to utility bills, students might want to alternate months, or develop a system where one roommate pays the bills

Splitting the Phone Bill

The phone bill can be a little tricky, because it's a shared service, but the potential exists for one roommate to account for two-thirds of the bill. Let's say two roommates receive a $70 phone bill for September—$38 for basic services/local calls and $32 for long distance. Here's an example of one way to break it down.

1. The base bill is really $38 ($70–$32), so each roommate should pay half that amount ($19), plus his personal toll calls.
2. $32 of the bill is for individual toll calls—$24 for Roommate 1 and $8 for Roommate 2.
3. Roommate 1 would owe $43 ($19 + $24), and Roommate 2 would owe $27 ($19 + $8).
4. Roommate 1 could then pay the phone bill, and Roommate 2 could write him a check for his share, or vice versa.

and is reimbursed for the roommate's share. However it's worked out, be sure it's fair to everyone.

Keep in mind similar circumstances where one roommate should pay more than her share of a utility bill. If you live in an off-campus apartment for the summer and are billed for electricity, a student who uses an air conditioner regularly in her room should volunteer to cover at least 60 percent of the bill if her roommate doesn't use one—maybe an even higher percentage. It's something the second student might feel awkward bringing up, but that doesn't mean it won't bother her. When a $200 bill hits the mailbox in July, a 50–50 split is unfair.

Despite students' emphasis on fairness, it's rarely possible to split everything perfectly. If you and your roommate together spend $45 on shared groceries one day, for example, consider asking for $20 up front, and forgetting about the extra $2.50. You'll send a subtle message that the big picture—general fairness—is more important than splitting everything with utmost precision. Next time, your roommate might round it off in your favor. (If your roommate insists on that precision each time, though, don't complain. At least you'll never be shortchanged.)

Sean Carroll (University of Illinois at Urbana–Champaign, Class of 2004) kept this in mind when he moved into an off-campus apartment with two friends. "Upon moving into our apartment, my roommates and I established what I liked to call 'our little Communist paradise' and we split everything among the three of us. For bills, this made perfect sense since we all used the apartment just as much as the other. As for food, it seemed too petty to split up every little thing each of us bought, and in the long term it would probably be rather equal anyway. This kind of system works out very well as long as all roommates are in agreement with the system."

How will I get used to the relative lack of privacy?

Like many issues covered in this book, privacy is a matter of perspective. College, despite an overflow of youth and energy, can be excruciatingly lonely for those far away from home who haven't yet adjusted. For them, the solution lies in knowing that there's always someone in the floor's lounge watching TV, or there's always a door to knock on—or walk on through, since they're often propped open.

Conversely, for those who are adamant in their desire to be left alone, a dorm full of freshmen will never be the place to find solitude. It's more like a beehive or a shopping mall where nobody over 21 is allowed.

So how do students deal with that lack of privacy? They get used to it. They learn to adapt. They make the most of it. And the best ones thrive on it.

"I not only got used to the lack of privacy, I loved it," said Vinda Rao of Tufts University. "Some of my best memories of freshman year were of me spending time in other people's rooms, watching movies, eating burnt popcorn, and instant messaging. You'll get used to having your door open—in fact, it'll seem kind of strange if it's closed, other than when you're asleep."

Fortunately, as Vinda points out, students do have control over their privacy: "If you are an extremely private person, lock your door, and [when you do want to socialize] spend time in the common area." Doing so is a great way to get to know people, she says.

The privacy crunch is felt most acutely by those who live in small, open rooms with a roommate. Jennifer Maden of the University of Tennessee, Knoxville, suggests learning your roommate's schedule, and taking advantage of the time that she'll be out at class, work, or activities. "These times are good to set aside if you know that you need alone time on a weekly basis. Otherwise, the privacy issue becomes less important over time."

Your room, however, is not the only place to find privacy. There will be days when you want to be alone but your roommate is likely going to be in the room all day, watching TV, reading, or surfing the Web—such as on a rainy Sunday. In these cases, if you really want privacy, you'll have to find it somewhere else.

> *"You are living with someone in a relatively small space. That doesn't mean that you have to always be around someone 24/7. Go to the library or the student union to read or have some alone time. Go for a run or to the gym alone. There are plenty of ways to get away from the perpetual slumber party that is college when you need it."*
>
> —Anisa Mohanty, University of North Carolina at Chapel Hill, Class of 2007

As important as alone time is, however, Jennifer Maden advises being grateful for the positive aspects of sharing a room: "You learn to appreciate having someone to talk to when you get home at 2 a.m. as opposed to being by yourself, or the fun of watching TV with another person."

Erika Brant (Northern Arizona University, Class of 2006) remembers one lack-of-privacy issue in college life she had to get used to in a hurry: "The big adjustment was a community shower," she remembers. "It was weird having to wear flip-flops every time you showered and having to walk down a long hallway in a robe or towel, often past groups of people, just to get to the bathroom. Eventually, you just get used to it and before you know it, you don't even think about it."

How can I deal with the roommate from hell?

From her own experiences and those she's gained as a Resident Assistant at Northern Arizona University, Erika Brant knows that talking things out is most often the best solution to roommate disputes. Open discussion, she says, is a catalyst for positive change; once both sides hear what the other has to say, they can forge a compromise to satisfy each other's requests. It may not result in the pair becoming best friends, but it frequently fosters a peaceful coexistence.

She also knows that occasionally it doesn't work out. "Sometimes it is impossible for roommates to get over conflicts and the only solution is to separate them," she says.

It's a last-resort solution for many schools, only considered after multiple meetings with R.A.s, hall directors, and other officials have failed. Because the college must negotiate which student leaves the room and find a new place for that student, they prefer to avoid the hassle by getting the conflicted students to work it out. Many schools won't even consider a roommate-change request in the first few weeks of the semester because so many roommates think their dispute is impossibly intractable.

It helps to know if you're a legitimate candidate for a roommate change. "There is a major difference between a roommate from hell and one that you just don't like," says Brian Bamberger (University of Illinois at Urbana–Champaign, Class of 2006). "There are roommates you don't get along with and wouldn't really socialize with—but they don't do things that just make your life a nightmare."

A language and culture barrier, opposite tastes in music—music his roommate never played softly—and some old-fashioned stubbornness made for a miserable first year for Mike (Columbia University, Class of 2005).

How to Tell If Your Roommate Is from Hell

If your roommate snores sometimes, wakes you in the middle of the night on occasion, and is habitually messy, congratulations—you have a typical college roommate and will likely receive little sympathy if you request a room change. You might have a case, however, if the roomie:

- ✓ Regularly disrupts your ability to sleep or study at all hours of the day, and refuses to make changes
- ✓ Engages in illegal activities
- ✓ Smokes, and you don't
- ✓ Endangers you physically in any way
- ✓ Interferes with your practice of religion

After months of spats and miscommunication, Mike returned to the room one day to find his roommate installing a large speaker system in the center of their small double room. He knew it was the last straw. The relationship had failed. But both guys were obstinate. Neither wanted to move out, because at that point in the year, the other would likely reap the extra benefit of getting the entire room to himself. They ended up partitioning the room, with a flag improvised as a barrier between the two sides. They didn't communicate, and both tolerated the uncomfortable arrangement for the rest of the school year.

Anisa Mohanty suggests that if you're stuck in a bad situation, do your best to persevere and try not to make a bad situation worse. "Don't be equally obnoxious just out of spite," she says. "Let it go. Perhaps you can switch roommates . . . otherwise, put your headphones on and do your thing. Or go hang out elsewhere."

This isn't to suggest that you should avoid your room all the time. You live there and should feel free to come and go as you please. At the same time, however, if you're stuck with a roommate you really can't stand, and the relationship has broken down, it's healthier for you to minimize the time you spend with the other person. Even if the two of you can't stand each other, you both might agree to scheduling time to be in and out of the room, because it benefits both of you.

Fortunately, it rarely reaches this point. "While many people fear the roommate from hell, it is a pretty rare occurrence—or at least in my experience," says Brian Bamberger. "Only one of my friends has ever had major problems with his roommate. Most roommates get along fairly well—or at least don't do anything drastic to make living together a nightmare."

Where to go if your roommate is unbearable? Try these places:

- ✓ Other friends' rooms (but don't overstay your welcome)
- ✓ Library
- ✓ Student activity center
- ✓ Gym
- ✓ Computer lab
- ✓ Common areas

4

Food

Dorm food isn't as bad as it is put out to be. And, in the first two weeks of the semester, you may actually enjoy the food. But, after those first two weeks, you'll start missing those home-cooked meals that mom makes–and long for something other than dorm food.

—Brian Bamberger, University of Illinois, Class of 2006

You've heard of the phrase "feast or famine"? That could apply to the first month of a college freshman's diet.

Why feast? Four words: All you can eat. Enough said.

Why famine? The food may be fine, but don't expect home cooking. Finicky eaters may be in for a rough ride.

Unlike at home, where a big refrigerator holds most of your favorites every day, the options are, in some ways, more limited at school. There's the dining hall, where most freshmen eat most of their meals; the limited food items students keep in their dorm rooms; and restaurants and fast-food joints located around campus.

Since it's not practical to cook much in your dorm, and it's not really affordable to eat in restaurants regularly, dorm dwellers tend to eat most of their meals in the dining hall—for better or worse, feast or famine. This chapter explores how students manage to eat what they want, take advantage of what's available, and stick to a reasonably healthy diet.

What are usually the best choices in the dining hall?

Welcome to the dining hall, where the food is plentiful, the cups and plates are unbreakable, and the servers seem to use ice cream scoops to dish out everything from peas to potatoes to stuffing—it's something to do with consistent portion sizes, we're told.

The good news: Of the dozens of students asked about their dining hall experiences at schools around the country, only a few truly pan it. Almost all agree that the dining hall is what you make of it.

In other words, those who eat pizza and french fries every day will probably complain about the offerings, even as they start packing on the pounds as a result. Those who try different things on the menu and don't expect a gourmet meal every time they sit down usually find the food to be pretty decent.

Brian Bamberger (University of Illinois at Urbana–Champaign, Class of 2006) says there's always something good to eat in the dining hall, although it often involves looking beyond the main hot dish. "The salad bar, sandwich bar, and cereal selections can salvage any meal. These often-healthier options allow for variety that won't make you tired of eating the same thing day in and day out."

Students repeatedly cite the salad bar as an example of making the most of your meal plan. And they're not talking about just lettuce, tomatoes, and a scoop of dressing.

> *"The key is to learn to spice them [salads created from the salad bar] up. Say, for instance, it's lunch and they are serving grilled chicken sandwiches. Ask for a couple of the breasts, but no bun. Cut up the chicken and you have yourself a ready-made chicken salad without spending $5 at Wendy's. Also, deli meat can be cut up to make chef salads."*
>
> —Tom Brenner, University of Michigan at Ann Arbor, Class of 2005

You probably won't find finely prepared mixed-ingredient salads in your dining hall, and even the most extensive salad bar may not easily impress. But by taking the time to customize your meal, you can find something that matches your tastes and is healthy at the same time.

One student at American University tells how she takes fresh spinach, when it's available, sprinkles it with some olive oil, salt, and pepper, and pops it in the microwave for a minute to get fresh-cooked spinach. "Don't be too scared to try new things—tacos from the vegan section or even the soup," she suggests. "Sometimes you strike out, but other times you find something you would actually have twice."

That extra initiative in the dining hall really does pay off, says Irene Fernando (University of Minnesota, Twin Cities, Class of 2007). "The whole idea of making the best out of each situation is called into play," she says. "Learn what you like and try to add your own spin on it. Really optimize your utility—if they have cooked vegetables one day, take the effort to go to the salad bar and throw some cheese on it. Pop it in the microwave while you get your drinks, and trust me—it will taste good. Remember: In college, the microwave is your friend."

Most Consistent Bets in the Dining Hall

These foods are consistently good in dining halls, and have the added bonus of being healthy, if you watch how you prepare them:

Bagels	They may not be as good as the fresh baked ones at the corner deli back home, but put them in the toaster and add your favorite spread, and they're a good substitute.
Sandwiches	At lunch time, skip past the hot-food line, grab a roll (try toasting it), and customize a sandwich for yourself. This is another category where you can come close to replicating a classic from the neighborhood deli. If you're "low-carbing" it, you can avoid the roll and just eat the deli meats and toppings.

Salad bar	It's the perfect place to customize your meal. With dozens of ingredients, from green peppers to chick peas, available, it's easy to make a different salad you'll enjoy just about every day.
Fresh fruit	Many schools will allow you to take a piece back to your room after dinner.
Cereal	Guaranteed to taste just like home. "I've seen hamburgers floating in fat, cooked-to-death vegetables, and bland sauces—but the cereal and fruit are always good. I have yet to find a dining hall that can screw those two things up," says Kristina Ihlenfeldt, a 2003 graduate of Clemson University.
Cheese	The only item on this list that's unavoidably fatty, it will add lots of gooey flavor to vegetables, chicken, sandwiches, or baked potatoes. Use it sparingly to rescue a bland dish, or as an occasional treat.
Baked potatoes	The Atkins folks have made the poor spud Public Enemy No. 1. But if you're gaining weight in college, it positively won't be because you're having a modestly garnished baked potato with your dinner a few nights a week.

What food options will I have besides the dining hall?

On plenty of occasions, you won't be around the dining hall at mealtime. Whether you're working, studying at the library, or just plain don't feel like it, you'll have to figure out where your next meal is coming from.

You'll find plenty of options on the main campus drag at most schools, with shops and restaurants catering to college students' tastes and budgets, such as Marshall Street at Syracuse University, Franklin Street at the University of North Carolina at Chapel Hill, or High Street at Ohio State University.

Pizzerias and burger joints, plus ethnic specialties such as Mexican and Chinese food restaurants, are almost always located right on campus. They don't offer much in the way of health food, but for price and convenience, they're tough to beat. Many students prefer the comforts of brand-name franchises such as McDonald's or Domino's, but others, such as Sean Carroll (University of Illinois at Urbana-Champaign, Class of 2004), say it's worth trying everything on campus. He says he's found some good places by taking this approach, and saved some money in the process: "Some of the best deals—and pizza—come from the places you would have never heard of before," he says.

Tom Brenner (University of Michigan at Ann Arbor) agrees that savviness pays off for budget-conscious college students. For example, he's found a cheap burrito café that's popular with Michigan students, especially late at night. "These sorts of places—with $1 quesadillas and the like—are critical to surviving on a college budget," he says.

And it's easy to keep enough basics in your room to make a simple entrée or small meal. Jacqueline Victor (University of Colorado at Boulder, Class of 2006) keeps food for snacks as well as meals in her dorm fridge. She typically prepares two to three meals a week on her own, depending on her level of satisfaction with the dining hall options. And sometimes she brings her own items to the dining hall to complement an otherwise plain dish—for example, she occasionally brings avocados to liven up sandwiches.

> *"I make a bi-weekly trip to the grocery store to furnish my refrigerator with entrees, snacks, and drinks, such as pre-prepared food, sushi, soup, fruit, vegetables, ice cream, popsicles, string cheese, cereal, iced tea, milk, and juice."*
>
> —Jacqueline Victor, University of Colorado at Boulder, Class of 2006

While the dining hall may not provide haute cuisine every night, the alternatives may not be as appealing as they seem. Students who regularly bypass the dining hall usually end up either buying fast food, such as hamburgers, pizza, and Chinese take-out, or they cook the basics in their dorm by making Ramen noodles, macaroni and cheese, Hot Pockets, and microwaveable frozen entrees, says Erika Brant (Northern Arizona University, Class of 2006). Those foods are all good on occasion, but a steady diet of them often leaves students yearning for the kind of food diversity they can only find in the dining hall—the option they tried to get away from in the first place.

"Most residence halls have kitchens, but having to take all of your stuff to the kitchen and having to wait for your food to cook is usually a huge hassle," Erika says. "Some students come to college planning to cook every night. Usually the cooking routine lasts a week before those students start looking for a different option."

For those who don't want to cook, and don't want to leave their rooms, there's always the option of ordering food in. But that option, too, can get old fast—especially if it's relied upon too frequently.

Irene Fernando (University of Minnesota, Twin Cities, Class of 2007) knows the dangers of getting in a dining rut. She suggests an occasional departure from the routine of the dining hall, fast food, and late-night noodle soup. "One of my personal faves was this place called Village Wok, and a buddy of mine and I like, lived there," she says, speaking of her freshman year.

> *"You and a friend—or even a group of friends—should go out and eat a real dinner every now and again. And by eating dinner with your friends, I do not mean bringing your own 'Easy Mac' to their dorm room and using their microwave and water."*
>
> —Irene Fernando, University of Minnesota, Twin Cities, Class of 2007

If you're looking to downsize your dining hall plan, breakfast is a good meal to eat in your room instead—especially if you're a cold-cereal-and-juice kind of person. Like many students, Sean Carroll (University of Illinois at Urbana–Champaign) prefers eating breakfast in his room to heading over to the dining hall. He makes sure he always has milk in the fridge and cereal in his closet. The cost is minimal, and he's not paying a nickel for all the hot breakfast foods in the dining hall that he's not eating anyway.

Cold cereal in the room is one of those rare win-win situations: In addition to being cheap and convenient, it's also a healthy choice, especially if you don't overdo it on the sugar-coated cereals. It's incredibly easy to prepare, anytime. And most cereals are good sources of vitamins and are low in calories.

Realizing that students want more options outside of the dining hall, many colleges and universities have struck deals with fast-food chain restaurants, where students' dining dollars or meal-plan points can be redeemed at on-campus food courts. The new food court in the Stamp Student Union Building at the University of Maryland, for example, offers Chick-Fil-A, Taco Bell Express, and Panda Express Asian Cuisine.

The University of Illinois at Urbana-Champaign has Blimpie, Sbarro, and Sushi San, among others. These choices break up the monotony of traditional dining hall fare, says Illinois student Brian Bamberger, who adds a caveat: "While these options are good, don't get into the habit of utilizing it all the time, or the 'freshman 15' will be soon acquired."

How can I avoid the "freshman 15"?

You've heard about it.

And sure, you dismissed it.

But—like term papers and late nights—the "freshman 15" is a reality for new college students.

Not all of them, of course. There will always be the fortunate ones who eat everything on the menu and don't gain a pound. But they're the exceptions. You're the rule.

For those who haven't heard of it, the "freshman 15" refers to the 15 pounds that many college students gain in their first year away at school. Some classic reasons for this:

- ✓ Those four words noted in the introduction to this chapter—"all you can eat"—can really catch up to you. Just because you can eat it, your body doesn't necessarily need it. What it doesn't need is turned to fat.
- ✓ College students are often under lots of stress, keep lousy hours, and are suckers (we mean that in a nice way) for daily doses of cheap, convenient, fattening foods. Late-night chicken wings, a steady diet of pizza and french fries, and regular study-break milkshakes are delicious, convenient, comfort foods that are guaranteed to help you pack on pounds if eaten regularly.
- ✓ Alcohol always catches up to you. If it's not in the form of a splitting headache the next morning, it might also happen after a few weeks of regular drinking, when you notice your pants are a little tighter than they used to be.
- ✓ Former high school athletes who aren't part of a team anymore may get heavier if they don't find a way to make up for the exercise they're missing. "If you eat the same now as you did when you played three sports all year, needless to say, you will probably gain weight," says Kristina Ihlenfeldt of Clemson University.

Emily Bott (Utah State University, Class of 2006) never reached the "15" plateau, but she was surprised when she found herself approaching it during her freshman year. "When I first started school, I don't think I realized I was eating badly," she recalls. "I was getting all the food that I thought would be good to eat, and then by midsemester I noticed that I was in fact gaining some weight. I think I started gaining weight because after class, when I was bored, I would come home and just eat."

Once she noticed she was gaining weight, she devised an effective two-part counterpunch: She began using her bike regularly around campus, and started eating a greater variety of foods, diversifying from her peanut-butter-and-jelly routine. It worked.

As Emily's experience shows, the first step to beating the freshman 15 is to acknowledge that it exists. This way, you'll think twice before you eat your third burrito in as many days. Of course, even after thinking twice, you still might scarf it down. Who can blame you? You're hungry, it's late at night, and it's college. But at least you'll know that you should make an extra effort to work it off the following day. In the absence of that frame of mind, it's very likely that you'll join the ranks of overweight freshmen.

> *"Just use your head. Pizza and ice cream . . . cause weight gain, so stay away from them. Opt for lean meats and veggies and drink plenty of water. It's all there—you just have to make the choice of what to eat."*
>
> —Jessica Bal, University of Connecticut student

Erin Fletcher (Duke University, Class of 2004) says those who ate well before going away to school should be able to continue that approach. If it worked at home, she reasons, it'll work at school. "It's hard to keep the same sort of schedule and consistency, but it's the best way to avoid gaining weight and overindulging," she says. "You didn't go to the store after every dinner and buy half a pound of gummies and M&Ms before, so don't do it now."

Valerie Rozycki (Stanford University, Class of 2005) has also been mindful of the "if-it-works-at-home" approach. "I used to never eat desserts at home just because we rarely had them in the house," says Valerie. "All of a sudden when the dining hall offers brownies 24/7, I started eating them more frequently, and it began to show." She's since switched to a healthier alternative—frozen yogurt.

A key component to any weight-loss or weight-maintenance plan is exercise, the benefits of which far exceed burning off fat. Melinda Stiles (University of Minnesota, Twin Cities, Class of 2007) found that regular exercise solved her stress problems a lot better than junk food. "After the first few weeks, I started to get really busy and stressed. I found that after I went out for a run, I felt less stressed, ate better, and, consequently, kept the weight off," she says.

Smart choices in the dining hall also helped her keep her weight in line. "It's hard to decide what to eat when there are so many options, but I tried to remember that I didn't always have to eat until I was full every time."

Melinda put her approach to the test during one rough stretch when she stopped exercising and didn't pay attention to her food choices. The inevitable occurred: "The pounds started creeping on," she remembers, before providing a word of caution to new students: "Make sure to keep up on exercise!"

> *"I walked everywhere my freshman year. I rarely took the bus, and I joined club sports teams—that was a great way to meet new people and stay in shape."*
>
> —Mela Kirkpatrick, University of North Carolina at Chapel Hill, Class of 2004

The best results occur, of course, when students exercise and make smart diet choices. By not eating too much food and limiting junk food, regular exercise will work to keep your body toned—in tip-top shape—rather than merely keeping the flab off.

This doesn't mean that you can't enjoy that cheeseburger and fries. But it's best to make those indulgences an occasional, rather than routine, part of your life.

Eight Ways to Deep-Six the "Freshman 15"

1. **Hit the gym.** Many colleges have invested in modern fitness centers with state-of-the-art equipment, basketball courts, tracks, and weight rooms. Your student ID is all you need to get in.

2. **Use your feet.** Depending on where you went to high school, it's possible that you'll do more walking now than you ever have, especially if you're attending a school with a big campus. Resist the temptation to take a shuttle bus when you could instead take a 10-minute walk. Going to the fourth floor? Take the stairs instead of elevators—always. Use extra minutes on campus to walk off part of your lunch.

continued

Eight Ways to Deep-Six the "Freshman 15" (continued)

3. **Don't overdo it at the buffet.** One plate of food should do the trick at most meals.

4. **Make smart food choices.** Some substitutions can drastically cut down on your calorie and fat intake. Pretzels instead of potato chips; turkey breast instead of ham and cheese; ice water instead of Coke; frozen yogurt instead of ice cream. A savings of 100 or 200 calories a day can help you maintain your weight or even drop a few pounds.

5. **Easy on the desserts.** Expect an assortment of pies, cakes, puddings, and ice cream in the dining hall. Indulge yourself on occasion, but doing so every day can be habit- and fat-forming.

6. **Easy on the late-night snacks.** This is another habit that can really inflate your waistline. Why? By eating superfatty foods right before going to bed, you're eating the worst foods at the worst possible time. Your body won't be doing any movement to shake off all those calories. Try to limit the late-night pizzas or chicken wings.

7. **Watch what you drink.** If, in your first year at college, you eat the same and exercise the same as last year, yet you drink more, guess what's going to happen?

8. **Figure out what works for you.** You'll probably have a friend who eats like a linebacker and exercises like a cow yet remains as skinny as a string bean. Or maybe that person is you. Find out what you need to do to manage your weight. Do this by monitoring your weight, your food choices, and your exercise plan, and making adjustments as you need them. Some people will need to work harder than others to stay trim.

5

Academics

> *Don't put undue pressure on what classes you take. Just understand that what you take now decides what you take later in terms of prerequisites and time restrictions.*
>
> —J.C. Ratigan, Texas Christian University, Class of 2007

You mean I have to go to class, too?

That might be the reaction of some students after the whirlwind experience of their first few days on campus. So much happens upon arrival—from meeting your roommate and floormates to experiencing your first dining hall meal, and from learning your way around campus to setting up your dorm room—it can be easy to overlook the academic part.

After a series of rapid-fire adjustments that might shock your system, this is the big one—the reason you packed your bags and headed out to school in the first place. This chapter will explore some of the basics as students start digging into schoolwork: choosing classes, setting up a schedule, developing study habits, and dealing with the rigors of college-level assignments.

What classes should I take?

Faced with a catalog of hundreds or thousands of courses from which to choose, it's no wonder that freshmen often don't know where to start when it comes to selecting classes. Most freshmen follow one of these paths:

✓ **Focus entirely on required classes, to get them out of the way first.** This choice ensures you'll be out in front on essential coursework, and able to focus on your major in your sophomore, junior, and senior years. You'll also be able to take the maximum number of upper-level electives when you have more room on your schedule.

✓ **Take the classes that interest you and worry about requirements later.** This guarantees that you'll enjoy courses that address your interests, though many upper-division classes have prerequisites that keep freshmen out. This approach has the potential to help students who don't know what they want to major in yet. Ultimately, though, it will remove elective class choices from junior and senior year, when most students are itchier to try classes outside the mainstream. Many schools do have some kind of liberal arts foundation requirement, so a safer bet for the undecideds may be the one below.

✓ **Take mostly required classes, but include one elective—two at most.** This allows you to get started on your core requirements and also satisfy your curiosity about subjects that are intriguing but not required.

Not surprisingly, different approaches work well for different students.

"My first semester, I chose classes that I thought I should be taking for my major as well as a class that I was purely interested in," said Minal Ahson (University of Miami, Florida, Class of 2005). "After meeting with my adviser, I figured out that I was on the right track, and future semesters I was more informed when making decisions on classes."

Although Minal is majoring in microbiology and religious studies, she's been able to take coursework in other areas she's interested in while fulfilling requirements. "I hope to someday attend medical school, so I am taking the opportunity to learn about art history and political science—two of my interests—now as an undergrad." The mixture of classes she wants to take and needs to take, combined with the expertise of her adviser, has helped her stay on track.

Faculty advisers not only can help you select the right courses, they also can help you make sure you're on schedule to graduate. Their value is something most students agree on. "I highly recommend talking with an academic adviser and nailing down classes you need to fulfill graduation requirements," says Shane K. Lee, a student at California State University, Long Beach. "Once you have this framework, see if there are fun classes that you want to take that will fulfill these requirements."

Jennifer Maden (University of Tennessee, Knoxville, Class of 2004) has a friend who learned the importance of advisers the hard way. The friend "never saw an adviser and thought that if he took 120 hours of classes he could graduate," she recalls. The friend took entry-level classes for his first two years before he was told he'd have to follow some sort of formal program—including upper-division classes—to earn a diploma.

Not choosing a major until sophomore year is nothing unusual—but if you haven't gotten your requirements mostly out of the way by the end of that year, it's possible you'll have to stay at school an extra semester or year to complete them. Considering the time and costs involved, it's something most students prefer to avoid.

Students don't necessarily need to have their four years mapped out in the fall of freshman year, but they do need a game plan. They need a starting point to work from—something to adjust, and keep track of, as they navigate towards deciding a major. Most colleges have a suggested approach for freshmen who have not declared their majors. Those who follow that course will be ready when they do declare a major, hopefully by the end of their sophomore year. Those who don't are more likely to meander and eventually waste time by taking classes that won't count towards degree requirements.

Brigham Young University even offers a class that helps students choose a major and career. Matt Baker (Class of 2005) wishes he had taken that class during his freshman year. "After two years of college, I finally enrolled in that class," he says. "It helped me finally decide on the major I am now pursuing. I only wish I would've done that sooner because I think I could've saved a lot of time and money by doing so."

When a student isn't quite sure what to major in, it can be tough to fill out the course schedule. There's a temptation to try a little bit of everything.

Students who opt for elective classes their first semester may very well meet with success, but they should proceed with caution, says Jennifer Maden. "First of all you must remember to think about if the classes will actually take you to a career or major. Don't just take poetry, karate, and history of music because they all sound interesting—try to actually take classes that will lead you to a major."

"For example," Jennifer says, "those who are seriously interested in one subject area should go ahead and take a class in it [again, a prerequisite may stand in the way]. If it turns out that the course was good, and the potential is there to turn it into a major, they can try to do that. And if the class didn't spark any lasting interest, at least it helped rule out a subject area that could have been a major choice."

Brian Bamberger (University of Illinois at Urbana–Champaign, Class of 2006) has found success by taking a range of classes that interest him while also satisfying requirements. "I have found that taking courses in a variety of fields is best, and the most enjoyable," says Brian, who's majoring in biology and music education. "My first semester, I took molecular and cellular biology, anthropology, mathematics, chemistry (lab and lecture), and band. The diversity of the subjects allowed my semester to be enjoyable and interesting. Sometimes having too much of one thing is bad."

He's continued that approach in subsequent semesters at Illinois, taking coursework in Spanish, chemistry, art and design, and mathematics.

The biggest advantage to getting requirements out of the way early is that it frees students to dig into their major as well as unique class offerings in their junior and senior years. During the early semesters of focusing on requirements, students get to know professors, departments, and other students—all of whom help them decide the best electives to take.

While advisers are great with the formalities of choosing classes and following a degree program, they might not be the first to tell you if one of their colleagues isn't the greatest teacher of English lit. Instead, the best source for information about classes taught by specific instructors is other students.

What to Ask Upperclassmen About Courses You're Interested in Taking

- ✓ Would you recommend this course overall?
- ✓ What's the workload?
- ✓ How good is the professor? How does the professor compare with others who have taught the same course? Is he or she accessible? Fair?
- ✓ How tough is the grading?
- ✓ How relevant is the material to what I'm interested in as a career choice?

"Upperclassmen are great resources," says Minal Ahson. "They will give the most candid answers about classes and professors."

No matter who you talk to, though, it can't hurt to get a second opinion about a course you're unsure of. Students may like or detest classes for reasons that have no bearing on what you might experience. If you're majoring in English and your buddy, the pre-med major, tells you that organic chemistry is a great class, she may be right—but she's predisposed to like such a class. It might be better to seek the opinion of fellow liberal arts majors who might approach the class from a perspective more like yours.

"If you're curious about a class, ask around," says Jessica Smith-Kaprosy (University of Wisconsin–Madison, Class of 2006). "Both good and bad classes develop reputations."

How many credits should I take in my first semester?

When starting off in college, some students—particularly the high achievers—take an aggressive approach, signing on for more coursework than they need in an effort to get ahead. Others register for only what they must do to stay on schedule for a four-year degree program. And others play it safe by taking one fewer class than usual, with the belief that a strong start in the grades department is more important than falling slightly behind schedule.

When it comes to this decision, it's not so much choosing which strategy to take, but rather realizing what kind of student you are. Only you know that. Each of the above options is ideal for some students, yet a poor choice for others. And the reasons don't always have to do strictly with academics.

Erika Brant (Northern Arizona University, Class of 2006) has seen students take a variety of credit loads, and is a strong advocate of the "stay-on-schedule" approach. "I watched some students, who only took 12 credit hours their first semester, struggle—not because the classes were too difficult," she says. "They struggled because they had too much free time and were not challenged enough. With all of their free time they got in the habit of goofing around all the time. When it came time to study, they didn't know how to focus."

Like many universities, Northern Arizona has a standard system where 120 credits are needed for graduation. It works out neatly so that students can take five 3-credit classes each semester, for eight semesters, to graduate in four years. Other schools require only four classes a semester; expect these to be more intense than at the schools that require five classes.

At schools with systems similar to Northern Arizona's, some students elect to take only 12 credits so that they can ease into the college experience. This may be a good choice for students who struggled at times academically in high school, but it's not the best choice for most students, as Erika's experience suggests. "Fifteen credit hours should keep a first-semester freshman busy enough to get into the college-studying mode yet prevent an overwhelming experience," she says, an approach supported by the experiences of many students, such as Tom Brenner.

Some students do take less than 15 credits, and it proves to be the right choice. That was the case for Kimble Rawls (University of Arkansas at Little Rock, Class of 2005). "I took 12 credit hours—I made a 4.0 and after that I've taken between 17 and 19 credit hours," she explains. She planned her degree program with help from the history and education departments at UALR, and could have graduated early if it wasn't for her student government responsibilities. "Being able to stay organized, and plan effectively, I was able to take a heavy course load."

> *"I took 15 [my first semester] and that was plenty. I would actually advise against taking less than 15 or 16, though. I have found that having more to keep me busy helps me structure my time and get things done. You don't want to have time to become the life of the party right off the bat."*
>
> —Tom Brenner, University of Michigan at Ann Arbor, Class of 2005

Erika Brant explained that she's seen what can happen at the other end of the spectrum: Those who take too many credits right away often end up exhausted and burned out. "If students are so overwhelmed their first semester, they'll fret returning in the spring because they'll hate college," she says.

> *"A student's goal should be to balance everything in a way in which they will have the time to enjoy their first semester. College truly is the time of one's life. It's all in planning and insuring that they are making time to enjoy themselves."*
>
> —Erika Brant, Resident Assistant at Northern Arizona University, Class of 2006

For those on the borderline, Shane K. Lee suggests signing up for the average number of classes. If it appears to be overwhelming, you can drop the class that's giving you the most trouble. *(See page 76-79 for more on the add-drop process.)*

How should I plan my schedule?

9:15 a.m.

That's when Jennifer Maden's English class started on Tuesday and Thursday mornings her first semester.

"I thought to myself, 'This is no problem because I have been getting up at 6:30 a.m. for the past 12 years of school,'" says Jennifer (University of Tennessee, Knoxville, Class of 2004).

It turned out to be a big problem.

"After the first day of class I had to change my schedule because I was late to class and so tired I was falling asleep in class," she recalls. "You see, I didn't think about myself or my new lifestyle. I love to sleep late in the morning—I just never did it on weekdays in high school because I knew I had to get up and go, or get into trouble. Well, in college there is no one calling your parents or your dorm room when you don't show up to class—instead you just get too far behind."

It took Jennifer only one late, groggy class to grasp the fact that sleep shouldn't interfere with schoolwork. That's something many students don't pick up on for four years. If you absolutely can't do without nine hours of sleep a night, and you also have a class at 9 a.m. the next morning, your choices are few: Go to bed by 11 p.m. the night before or do poorly in the class. In the future, you'd be wise to select classes that meet later.

Rise and Shine!

As painful as early-morning classes can be, there is a big benefit if you schedule all your classes early in the day—with the right scheduling, you can have the entire afternoon and evening free. By concentrating your class time in the morning, it makes it easier to study in the early evening because you've had such a long break during the day. It also provides a large block of time in which you can work a part-time job or participate in campus activities. It's tougher to do those things when your classes take place later in the day or are more spread out.

> If you bunch up your classes from roughly 10 a.m. to 2 p.m., be sure to leave yourself room for a lunch break. Note: Most dining halls allow students to pick up a boxed lunch on their way to class in the morning, as long as they make arrangements in advance.

"The key to setting your schedule is to know yourself," says Jennifer. "Stop and think what time of day you will get up without your mom nagging you, and set your classes for after that time, whether it is 8 a.m. or 12 noon."

Lots of students choose classes that meet at noon or after. "Avoid 8 a.m. and 9 a.m. classes like the plague," advises Anisa Mohanty (University of North Carolina at Chapel Hill, Class of 2007). But she acknowledges a reality of freshman life that makes her advice hard to follow: Lots of required classes are only offered around that time. That's another reason to get those requirements out of the way. It's easier for juniors and seniors to avoid early-morning classes, because advanced specialty classes for majors usually don't meet first thing in the morning. If you think you don't like 8:30 a.m. classes as a freshman, you'll hate them even more as a senior.

Tom Brenner takes a compromise approach at the University of Michigan at Ann Arbor, where he aims to schedule his classes between 10 a.m. and 2 p.m. "If a class is too early, then I don't get enough sleep and that can ruin my whole day," he says. "If a class is all by itself in the afternoon, it is incredibly easy to skip."

For the first semester, it might be best to try Tom's hours, keeping in mind that you may have no choice but to take an early class if that's the only time it's scheduled. This timetable provides a good foundation on which to decide what will work next semester—you'll have room to start your classes earlier, if you want, or even later.

Mela Kirkpatrick (University of North Carolina at Chapel Hill, Class of 2004) frequently changed her schedule: "Just experiment with different times," she says. "It took me almost four years to figure out what schedule suited me the best."

Study tonight—or find something else to do?

With countless options on campus, it's easy to get distracted from schoolwork. Most students have time blocked out on their schedules for classes, part-time jobs, activities, and studying. What tends to overlap everything is hanging out—having fun, partying, or just plain relaxing. Even if you're not the social type, it's hard not to be social when you live on a floor with 20 or 30 people who are similar to you in many ways (academically successful, going to the same school) yet diverse enough (different hometowns, majors) to keep it interesting.

On plenty of occasions you'll have to choose between studying and doing something with your friends. It's not a life-or-death choice, but it often involves sacrificing either schoolwork or a good time. While it's not easy to stay entirely on top of one's schoolwork, doing so is the best way to avoid being conflicted when such dilemmas arise.

"Evenings are for fun, so I try to study during the day," says Tom Brenner (University of Michigan). He does this by studying or reading, even if he only has a half-hour break between classes. Those little things make it easier for him to go out on any given night.

Dave Munson (University of Chicago, Class of 2005) says there's plenty of room to be serious about school and have a good time. "A nice blend of both" is how Dave describes his approach. "Take the time to head out for some social stuff, even if you do have an 8:30 the next morning—just don't do it the night before a midterm."

A surprisingly popular way that many students balance classwork and partying is by devoting one night to each on the weekend. That might be such a shock to some that it bears restating: It means spending a Friday or Saturday night on a date . . . with your biology textbook.

It's a lot easier than it sounds, and it seems to work well. Sean Carroll (University of Illinois at Urbana–Champaign, Class of 2004) took that approach whenever he had a Monday exam. He sees two benefits to Saturday-night studying: The obvious benefit is that he's doing schoolwork on a night that it would be otherwise neglected. The second, though, is that by staying in and taking it easy, he's better prepared to hit the books the following day.

A typical late Saturday night means that Sunday doesn't usually start until late morning or early afternoon.

> *"Some of my most effective study sessions have been on Friday nights. It's less stressful than cramming for a Monday exam on Sunday night and it gives me a reason to celebrate guiltlessly on Saturday."*
>
> —Vinda Rao, Tufts University, Class of 2006

"Even if you do not study on the night you stay in on the weekend you will be more well-rested than if you went out partying both nights on the weekend," he says. "Making a plan for your studying on that night is also a good idea—even if it only takes up about 20 minutes of your night, it's well worth it on Sunday when you get down to business."

He's taken this approach because he knows that too much partying can take its toll on one's grades. "You know you will be studying on Sunday probably all day anyways, but heading to happy hour two nights in a row can really put you in a bad position when it comes to your fatigue level."

What happens if I blow off an assignment?

Do you want the CliffsNotes answer to this question? Laurel Cooper (Duke University, Class of 2005) has it: "You'll have to deal with the consequences," Laurel says. "Talk to your professor about it. He or she might cut you some slack. MIGHT. Or maybe she or he will fail you. That's just how it goes in college."

Laurel knows what she's talking about. The only thing certain about blowing off an assignment is that you're leaving your fate—whether it's 5 percent of your grade or 50 percent—in someone else's hands. It's a most uncomfortable feeling, with good reason: The blown-off assignment very often ends up as a zero grade.

Two aspects of blowing off assignments make it especially painful to receive that zero:

- ✓ The assignment's usually something you could have taken care of if you started it earlier. Think about it: Students don't look at their class syllabus and say to themselves, "Nah, I don't think this paper is for me" a month before it's due. It's more likely that they procrastinated until it was too late, and then couldn't find the time to get it done at the last minute. Or they didn't realize that professors mean business when they set a due date. Some professors make no distinction between papers handed in a day late and those never handed in—both get zeroes.
- ✓ Grading approaches vary wildly, but it's not unusual to have only a handful of assignments each semester. Skipping one could easily drop your class grade by a full letter.

"Assignments are easy points," says Jessica Smith-Kaprosy, "The more points you have going into exams, the better you'll feel. They're also good practice. If you review the material when doing the assignment, that's less studying you have to do later."

It makes no sense to toss away those easy points. "It will come back to haunt you. Seriously," says Jessica Xan DeLoach (University of Arkansas at Little Rock, Class of 2006).

Deadline extensions are only given when students have a verifiable excuse, such as an illness, emergency, or religious observation. Otherwise, most professors won't even consider waiving penalties.

Kristina Ihlenfeldt (Clemson University, Class of 2003) saw a broad range of policies during her years at Clemson. "It's not like high school where all the teachers know you and you can usually persuade them to let you turn things in late," she says. "Usually, if you blow it off, you get a zero. Still, it all depends on the teacher. They all have their own policies for accepting late work. Some don't have problems with it—usually the minority. Some subtract a percentage for each day late, and some just give you a zero without a chance to make it up."

Some homework assignments are optional, which can put students in a bind—on one hand, the teacher must be recommending the activities for a reason; on the other hand, it might seem better to focus on the assignments that count toward one's grade. Jeremy Armstrong (Purdue University, Class of 2007) faced this situation in Chemistry 111. When he received the syllabus for the class, he saw that homework did not count toward the final grade.

A Few Words About Academic Dishonesty

Of all the mistakes students can make academically, the biggest is the decision to cheat. Whether it involves copying another student's answers, failing to cite sources in a term paper, or fabricating quotes for a journalism class article, academic fraud is a threat to the integrity of a college education. After all, would you want your taxes to be prepared by an accountant who cheated his way through school?

Colleges impose severe sanctions on those who deliberately misrepresent their academic work. A failing grade in the class is typically the smallest sanction; suspension or expulsion is also a possibility—especially for repeat offenders.

The key to maintaining one's own academic integrity is to respect others. That means citing the source of any ideas or unique information you present in any aspect of your collegiate output. If you have any doubts about whether to cite something, check with your professor before turning the work in. Remember: It is always better to attribute excessively than minimally.

Keep these other points in mind:

- ✓ Guard your own work when taking a test. If two exams are turned in with the same wildly incorrect answer to question 6, the professor may place both of you under suspicion.
- ✓ Just as the Internet has made it easier to submit fraudulent papers, it has made it easier for professors to catch such deceit.
- ✓ If you are temped to plagiarize, keep in mind that the penalty for being a day late with a paper is far less than what you'll face if you're caught cheating.

"My first thought was to not do it," says Jeremy. "That is what I stuck to. I had a good-enough knowledge of the material without needing to do the homework to do well on the tests and labs." He ended up missing an "A" by a small amount but stands by his strategy.

Does it matter if I attend lecture classes?

Brian Bamberger (University of Illinois at Urbana–Champaign) always attended his lecture classes, along with hundreds of other students, during his freshman year. Attendance wasn't taken, and there were no guarantees that his presence was going to boost his grade, but he went regardless. His diligence paid off, however—he received good grades and initially took the same approach to his two lecture classes the following semester. It turned out, though, that the instructors were not in the same league as his first-semester profs. Attendance at every single lecture suddenly didn't seem like a top priority. "I decided to skip lecture more often than not," he explains. "And, quite honestly, I noticed a decline in my performance in those two classes."

Brian's experience illustrates the paradox faced by many college freshmen: Lecture classes are not the best way to learn new material, but they're an ingrained part of the landscape at many institutions. It takes an especially strong professor to make lectures come alive and impart a significant lesson. When a lecture doesn't accomplish that feat, students weigh the consequences of bailing out, at least on occasion.

While it can appear to be the right move in some cases, it's nearly always the wrong move.

> *"My belief is that you're paying for class and you might as well go. It will take you three times as long to learn information from a missed class than if you had actually just gotten out of bed and gone."*
>
> —Erin Fletcher, Duke University, Class of 2004

"Some people do not attend lectures and still do well in the class—but these people are the exception rather than the rule," says Brian. "Even if you can learn everything from your textbook and would rather not wake up for that 8 a.m. Physics 101 lecture, professors have a tendency to teach some concepts and facts that are not in the book—and they often test on these."

Skipping lecture classes that didn't seem critical was a choice that backfired on Denelle Walker (Louisiana State University, Class of 2006) in her first semester. With no attendance records, and no one to rouse her into going to class, she was more likely to skip lectures than attend them. "I would skip some of my classes for weeks at a time, and sometimes I would even sleep through all of my classes and not think twice," says Denelle. She started thinking when it came exam time, however. "I found myself trying to read eight chapters in one night and drinking grande frappacinos and taking No-Doz to try to stay awake and focus on my studying."

It wasn't enough.

"When the semester ended and the grades came out, it wasn't a good time anymore," she recalls. She had awful grades, lost one of her scholarships, and faced an uphill climb to raise her grade-point average to a respectable level. With little other choice, she took an entirely different approach the following semester: She went to class every day, paid attention, and reviewed her notes when she got back to her room. She realized this was a much better strategy, and it allowed her to stay involved on campus, too. "By going to class, being attentive, and looking over my notes, it made studying for exams so easy because I was familiar with all the topics. My grades changed dramatically and I wasn't killing myself just to get by—it was less stress and better grades."

Not all professors are dynamic and captivating, but they are usually very smart. They know students are tempted to skip lectures, and they tend to reward the ones who opt to sit in the 300-seat hall on sunny September afternoons by giving them clues about what might be on the next quiz or exam—something that can't easily be gleaned by reading the course's textbook, as Brian Bamberger observes.

> *"I enjoyed skipping astronomy class so much that I made habit of it, and because the final grade was contingent on only two exams I thought I would be just fine," she says. "Exam time came around and I was studying myself into confusion every day for a solid week and a half. I did well in the course, but if you calculate the total time I spent with lecture notes in my hands, I might as well have gone to every class."*
>
> —Vinda Rao, Tufts University, Class of 2006

The thought of playing catch-up may not seem like such a deterrent to skipping class. A critical aspect of it, though, is that while you're catching up—usually at midterm or finals time—you're likely trying to do the same thing with three or four other classes. It can be overwhelming. And at 2 or 3 a.m., while you're buried in schoolwork, your conscience can't resist taunting: "If you had just spent an hour in September in class, when you had no other assignments due, you wouldn't have to be breaking your backside now, when you have five finals to prepare for and three papers to write."

Some students don't look at attending class as an academic decision; for them, it's a matter of money. "Unless I am sick or have a doctor's appointment, I am at class," says Charlie McGregor Austin, a student at Michigan State University. "This is your life; you need to become responsible. If you don't, college is just going to be one big waste of money for you."

Students who skip lecture classes obviously think they can learn the material better by reading it in a textbook. Tom Brenner says this isn't likely. In fact, he's found the opposite is sometimes true: "I have found that attending class means that you don't always have to read the textbook," he says. "Once you sit down with a college textbook, you will see that it is always better to go to class. I do not think that it is possible to skip class on a regular basis and not feel any ill effects."

When considering blowing off class, it really comes down to what you're able to learn from lectures and how your attendance might affect your grade. A reality, not just in college, but in life, is that sometimes just "being there" counts, whether you realize it right away or not.

It's one of those intangible things. The lessons might sink in, even if you don't immediately realize it. You might have a foundation for understanding the material, so that when you review for the final, or read your textbook, it all makes sense quickly. If you discuss the grade with your professor, and you can articulate points made during lectures in your conversation, it might tip a borderline grade in your favor. One thing's for sure: You can't be sure unless you go to class.

"It is so very common for people to complain about their grades and then tell you about how they only went to class once a week for a three-day-a-week class," says J. C. Ratigan of Texas Christian University.

How and when should I start planning for graduate education?

The phrase "it's never too early" applies to students considering graduate school of any sort, whether it's for a master of arts degree, law school, or medical school. Just like with choosing a major, however, it doesn't mean that students need to know exactly what they want to do at the start of freshman year. What it does mean is that they need to be aware, more than most students, of the impact of their freshman-year decisions and have some sort of rough plan in mind.

> *"If you think that you want to go to graduate or law school, the best thing that you can do is get the best grades that you can and take upper-level courses."*
>
> —Jessica Smith-Kaprosy, University of Wisconsin–Madison, Class of 2006

What impresses graduate and law school admissions counselors most is not so much a particular field of study as much as a challenging one that results in excellent grades. The American Bar Association, for example, does not recommend any specific major for undergraduates. Instead, it encourages a curriculum that focuses on analytic reading, writing, and research skills.

For example, the Association says that while some students have taken traditional paths to law school by majoring in history, English, philosophy, political science, economics, or business, others come with backgrounds in art, music theory, computer science, engineering, nursing, or education.

If you are interested in going on to law school, a pre-law adviser can help you choose the best strategy. She can work with you to gauge your interests and recommend classes that will best prepare you for the kind of law you want to study.

With medical school, a similar strategy is encouraged, although a greater emphasis is placed on the sciences.

Med schools typically require coursework in biology, math, chemistry, physics, and English, according to the Association of American Medical Colleges. "But keep your undergraduate experience well rounded by also studying humanities and the social sciences," the Association recommends. "The ideal physician understands how society works and can communicate and write well. Extracurricular experiences also are important. You may want to volunteer at a local hospital or clinic to gain practical healthcare experience."

Those extracurricular experiences not only can provide invaluable exposure to your field of interest, but they also can help you decide if the field is right for you. Nothing—no book, class, lecture, or interview—can provide the full picture of a profession like being immersed in one.

The reality of graduate education doesn't sink in for many students until it's time to face the alphabet tests that weigh heavily in the admissions criteria of many schools—namely the MCAT, LSAT, GMAT, and GRE.

"These tests are long and hard, and they take a lot of preparation in terms of studying and learning how the tests work," says Jennifer Maden, who is now pursuing her master of social work degree in Nashville through the University of Tennessee, Knoxville.

> *"If you know what you want to do, try to take internships or other experiences related to the field. If you're going into a science field, try to get a hospital internship, a job in a laboratory, or apply for research grants. If you're an art major, study abroad in France or Italy. If you're going into law, try to become involved in political campaigns, student government, or get a job at a law office. . . . All of these factors have added up to some of my friends getting into the top law, medical, and business schools in the country."*
>
> —Anisa Mohanty, University of North Carolina at Chapel Hill, Class of 2007

She took the Graduate Record Exam (GRE) in the fall of her senior year, but wishes she had taken it even earlier. "The earlier you take these tests, the longer time you have before your scores are due to grad school—so if you need to retake it, then you can," she says. Jennifer had a challenging fall semester her senior year, and that made it difficult to concentrate on the GRE. She studied roughly twice a week for a few hours in the three weeks before the test, using a Kaplan book and CD-ROM. She says her preparation was adequate but not ideal.

"I did not give myself time to retake the test in case I did poorly," Jennifer recalls. "If I could do it again I would have taken it during the summer before my senior year, when I wasn't busy with other classes, or at the very beginning of the fall of my senior year, and use the summer to study. I think it is important to allow yourself the opportunity to take it again if you need to—not so you can fail, but just to take some of the pressure off." Note that with the GRE, all test scores achieved within the last five years are reported to the schools you select. Although they are subject to change, similar policies exist for other standardized graduate-school tests.

If you're not sure of what you want to do regarding graduate education, you're probably like most freshmen. But that means you should explore your options. "Attend career fairs and events the campus will hold to give you information regarding the opportunities that are out there for you," suggests Jessica Xan DeLoach. Students who attend these events have the chance to meet with recruiters who can provide helpful insights.

It helps to keep in mind that students don't magically find all the answers at these events. Rather, the events stimulate curiosity and provide exposure. It's a one-thing-leads-to-another type of situation: A student who visits a "law day" event might start by asking a recruiter what's needed for admission, and then be impressed that the recruiter specializes in fighting for the citizenship rights of people facing deportation. That might lead to exploring programs in that area at law schools around the country.

Minal Ahson, a pre-med student at the University of Miami, Florida, found it helpful to attend a seminar for pre-med majors her first month at school. (Students who haven't formally declared may be permitted to attend such events upon request.) The session let her know whom she could talk to for help, and how to approach her studies in the field.

She's learned that despite being in a pre-med program, she still has the freedom to take a range of classes. "I have gotten to know many students who do things or take classes 'so it will look good for med school.' Of course, you want to look good to graduate schools, but you want yourself to be appealing as an individual, not as a resume," she explains. "By getting involved in many different areas of volunteer service, I have further confirmed my interest in a life of service. I am more passionate now than ever about becoming a doctor and being involved with public- and global-health issues. Also, by not limiting myself to the typical pre-med organizations, I have met amazing people and have had the opportunity to learn many new things. Mostly, I have learned a lot about myself through all of these different experiences. Without them, I would not be the same person that I am today."

6

Early Discontent

"There is no guarantee you'll love your university right away. In order to give your school your best shot, you should keep an open mind and be willing to learn and try new things."

—Erika Brant, Resident Assistant at Northern Arizona University, Class of 2006

Students' emotions can vary wildly during their time on campus, especially in the first year. The exhilaration of newfound independence can yield to spasms of homesickness in the same weekend.

The first weeks and months can provide plenty of contrasts—a fun dining hall meal with friends from your floor one night, and a crummy sandwich by yourself on the other side of campus the next night, when you get out of work late. You might have lots of carefree days in the warm September sunshine, then find yourself stuck inside for hours on end on cold dark December days, working on one term paper after the next—all the while wondering how you'll pay your credit-card bill.

This chapter will touch on some of the areas that frequently give students trouble during the first few turbulent months of school and show how students confront their problems.

How can I be more than a number to my school?

Many students cite joining student organizations and getting to know professors as the best way to make a big college seem smaller, and to feel a little less like a Social Security number.

If you're wondering why students sometimes feel like Social Security numbers, it probably won't be long until you see why. It's because at many schools, those numbers are the primary means of identification—not students' names. If you have a problem with your meal plan, for example, college representatives might ask for your Social Security number instead of your name, although many will eventually confirm your name.

When Brian Peterson (University of Minnesota, Twin Cities, Class of 2007) was a high-school senior in his hometown of Crookston, Minnesota, he served on the student council, was a member of a student-based volunteer group, and played tennis and basketball, to name some of his activities.

When he decided to attend the University of Minnesota, he was concerned that it might be tougher to find a niche, as several people had suggested to him. "I thought the large size of the school would make it harder for me," he recalls. "But I was wrong. I quickly learned about several of the existing organizations and ways in which I could become involved. I knew I was interested in getting involved in some sort of student government organization, and I found that I had several options and levels I could pursue. I ended up running for a position on my residence hall council executive board as the food and facilities chairperson. It turned out to be a great way to meet new people and to get involved right away."

Brian found it so easy to join different groups because that spirit of involvement is contagious on college campuses. With most groups, existing members are thrilled to connect with others who share the same interests. It's usually as simple as saying, "What's this group all about?" and a friendly face will be glad to provide the full story.

"A school like the University of Minnesota, or any college for that matter, will always have people with similar interests and have so many more opportunities if only you are willing to take initiative and go after them," says Brian, who didn't only join groups—

> **Random ID Codes Are Replacing Social Security Numbers on Campus**
>
> The identification of students by Social Security number appears to be on the way out at many schools. Hackers penetrated the records system at the University of Georgia, officials announced in early 2004, exposing the Social Security and credit-card numbers of 31,000 students and applicants whose names were entered in the system after August 2002. Around the same time at New York University, it was discovered that the Social Security numbers of hundreds of students were posted on an unprotected university Web page. NYU officials responded by announcing it would no longer use Social Security numbers in any way for student identification.
>
> Similar switches, not necessarily prompted by security breaches, have been made or announced at Texas A&M University, the Georgia Institute of Technology, the University of Northern Colorado, the University of Hawaii, and Marshall University, among others. However, the new systems at most schools will simply involve a new random code of numbers, letters, or both that will be unique to each student.

he also helped form one. (Chapter 9 details how Brian and three fellow freshmen started a new volunteer organization called Students Today Leaders Forever that's beginning to make an impact beyond the Minnesota campus.)

To avoid feeling like a Social Security number, or a randomly generated ID number, students strongly recommend taking that first step toward making connections on campus—asking a question, making a phone call, or attending a meeting. After that point, the going gets easier.

"Students have to let go of being afraid of trying something new . . . let it go and get out there and network," says Kimble Rawls (University of Arkansas at Little Rock, Class of 2005). "College is supposed to broaden your horizons and help you see things differently." Over the years, she has met many students who haven't even visited the student centers at their co leges. Kimble got involved at UALR, and ended up being named president of the university's Student Government Association.

"Go to the student center and check out the different programs, organizations, and businesses that will try and recruit you," she recommends. "Actively allowing your skills to develop will increase your success in college and in life." By getting involved in leadership programs at UALR, for example, she's been able to attend conferences that have helped her to meet a broad range of people and develop her skills.

Rebecca Wood (University of Memphis, Class of 2005) joined the marching/pep band and the United Methodist Campus Ministry. Being part of both groups gave her the chance to meet students and faculty at the university, and to take on leadership roles. "I will graduate from college knowing that I made a contribution to the University of Memphis," she says. "There are probably hundreds of organizations on your campus to choose from—find one or two that interest you and jump in."

"I found that even if I was slightly interested in an activity, it was worth checking out. That's how I got involved with the Residence Hall Association—I had a ton of fun! It's through getting involved that you can really network with people and be opened up to great opportunities. As a first-year student, I had the opportunity to lead a group of students to the NACURH (National Association of College and University Residence Halls) conference at St. Louis University. If I hadn't had the desire to get involved, that would have never happened."

—Melinda Stiles, University of Minnesota, Twin Cities, Class of 2007

At the University of Virginia, Michael Ann Bevivino says it's tough to feel like more than a number at a school with about 13,000 other undergraduates, but she accomplished that by becoming a docent at the University Art Museum her freshman year. This helped make her college world a lot smaller. She advises patience for those who don't find their niche right away: "I think that this is something that takes a little bit of time."

How can I thrive in a class with hundreds of other students?

Of all the academic shocks students face when they start college, the large lecture hall can be among the biggest. It's probably nothing like any other class you've ever taken. The professor talks . . . and you listen. Occasionally she will invite questions or pose one to the students, but nothing approaching a true dialogue ever happens. How can it with up to 500 or more people in the room?

Some students adapt well—they go to class, prepare in advance by reading the textbook, listen carefully to the lectures, and take good notes. But a feeling of disconnect can still persist. The remedies suggested by students have one factor in common: making an effort to get to know the people in the class, from the professor, to the teaching assistant, to fellow students.

Emily Bott (Utah State University, Class of 2006) struggled at the thought of freshman-year lecture classes. She wondered if the professors cared or if she'd ever get anything out of the experience in such huge rooms. She found out they did care, and that she did benefit from the classes.

"The thing that worked for me the best was talking to my professor the first day of class and just introducing myself to him," she remembers. "From then on I would come up to him after class and ask him questions that would better my understanding of the class and let my professor know how serious I was in taking this class and getting a good grade."

Shane K. Lee made the vast lecture halls at California State University, Long Beach, seem a lot smaller with what he describes as a simple but overlooked strategy: sitting in the front row. Doing so makes it easy to forget the hundreds of students behind you, because you never have to look past them to see the professor or her presentation. "It feels like you're being lectured to directly. It's also harder to fall asleep right in front of the professor. Even if attendance doesn't count, it does. If the professor sees you every class right in front, paying attention, you may get the benefit of the doubt if you have a borderline grade and the professor knows who you are."

And on those infrequent occasions when the professor poses a question to the masses, Shane suggests raising your hand if you know the answer. "Often . . . no one will answer—you can almost hear the crickets chirping," he recalls from experience. The professor may very well appreciate your enthusiasm.

Some might consider these suggestions "geekish," but that's only so if you are disingenuous, appear overly enthusiastic, or monopolize the professor's time. Showing your interest in a class is nothing you should have to defend.

How can I make the most of the add/drop process?

No matter how excited or unhappy you are about some of the classes on your schedule, your feelings won't be confirmed until after the class starts. You might immediately get good vibes from a professor teaching a class you were dreading—and even consider making the subject area your minor or concentration. Likewise, the person teaching the first class in the sequence for your major—a class you couldn't wait to take—could turn out to be a complete dud.

Nothing is guaranteed, but these truths tend to expose themselves early in the semester.

Fortunately, by adding and dropping classes, you can tweak your schedule so that it's just right for you. As simple as it sounds, adding and dropping can be complicated. While the process varies from school to school, here are some general aspects of it that many schools have in common:

✓ Adding a class is more difficult than dropping one. To add a class, you will likely need the approval of the course's professor or department, as well as your adviser's signature—and you'll have to make sure there's room in the class (perhaps the toughest part). To drop, you may need only one signature—or none at all.

- ✓ The add/drop process lasts only the first few weeks of the semester, after which point enrollment is sealed. If you fail the midterm and don't expect to do much better on the final, you can't drop the course, but you can withdraw. (For additional information on withdrawing, see the "Dropping/Withdrawing" chart on page 79.)
- ✓ The process can be a hassle because most other students are going through the same process at the same time. For example, the slot you'd like in that poetry class may not be available only because another student hasn't yet completed the paperwork to drop it.

Students recommend registering for more classes than you'll likely stick with. This way, you can easily drop one and not have to worry about adding another.

"Add before you drop," suggests Vinda Rao of Tufts University, where the "add" deadline precedes the "drop" deadline. "So don't go on a dropping spree too early, or you'll end up not having enough classes for the semester."

Anisa Mohanty wishes she followed that advice at the University of North Carolina at Chapel Hill: "One of my biggest mistakes was not signing up for enough extra hours to drop the most miserable class ever—I would've fallen under the undergraduate minimum-hour requirement. Don't try to be a trouper and tough out a difficult class. If it's giving you grief for the first week or two, it's likely not going to get better. Get out; save your GPA."

Anisa also suggests that students considering dropping classes continue going to them until they're certain they have a replacement lined up. This way, if they're unsuccessful at getting into another class, and they need to stick with the class they wanted to drop, they haven't lost further ground.

> *"The first couple of years I did not use the [add/drop] process at all, because I did not know what kind of class was best for me. Once I got this idea down, when I got to a class for the introduction, if it required certain things that I was not comfortable with, and I liked a different type of class better, I could drop that class and add another. This made the last two years of college much better because classes were much more aligned with the kind of classes I wanted to take."*
>
> —Sean Carroll, University of Illinois at Urbana-Champaign, Class of 2004

Persistence can pay off when trying to get into a class that you especially want or need. Simply trying to enroll through the usual means may not work. Check every day to see if there's an opening—skipping a day may mean another student gets your slot. It may help to try to meet with or at least e-mail the professor and see if she can pull any strings to get you in. Even if you're not on the list, show up at the class before it starts and explain your situation. "If you're lucky, and the professor is kind, a professor may keep a waiting list and open more seats for interested students," says Jessica Smith-Kaprosy (University of Wisconsin–Madison, Class of 2006).

Bill Andrichik (University of Notre Dame, Class of 2007) wishes he had exploited the add/drop process: "Don't do what I did and be afraid to use it," he suggests to new students. "As long as dropping a class will not put you behind schedule for graduation, drop it if it will help your GPA."

A word of caution: Be aware of the difference between "dropping" a class and "withdrawing." The terms may sound like they mean the same thing, but there is a major distinction as the following table shows:

Dropping	*Withdrawing*
Dropping a class means it vanishes from your transcript—it's as if you never registered for it, and obviously, you don't receive a grade. This can only be done during the first few weeks of the semester, when many students elect to sample classes they're not quite sure they want to take. Students who meet the drop deadline are usually eligible for at least a partial reimbursement of their tuition, if they paid on a per-credit basis.	Withdrawing from a class is typically done during the middle or toward the end of the semester, although it usually can't be done the last few weeks of class. Students who withdraw often do so because they know they won't be able to complete final class requirements or because they are headed toward an especially poor grade. Those who withdraw don't receive a grade, but the withdrawal (W) is noted on the transcript. Students who elect to withdraw may not receive a refund for the fees they paid to take the class.

While withdrawing from a class isn't necessarily bad—it might be advisable, for example, if you're about to receive a D in a class in your major—too many Ws on your transcript could tell potential employers that you're not reliable enough to finish what you start. File this under "things to talk about with my adviser" should you ever seriously consider withdrawing.

On the same subject, "incompletes" are a possibility if you are unable to meet the requirements of a course by the end of the semester and if you have a legitimate reason. Professors are usually reluctant to allow incompletes, and grant them (effectively providing an extension to submit final coursework) only in dire circumstances. An I will appear on your transcript, and it will count as an F in terms of grade points until the coursework is made up. If it's not done within the agreed timeframe, the I converts to an F.

Should I transfer if I don't like my college?

Lilian Doan experienced the peaks and valleys of college life during her first year. Her first semester was great, but a new reality dawned on her during the bitter winter days at the start of the second semester. "After football season, the first snowfall, and an awesome winter break at home, the real excitement of experiencing things for the first time had just vanished," she remembers. "It was at this time, coincidentally, that the snowfall really began to pick up and the sun seemed to stop shining for two months. I soon became disenchanted with Notre Dame on the whole, and felt as if the only way to be happy was to transfer—it became something that I thought about a lot."

She was scared to tell other people about her feelings, she recalls, because it seemed nobody felt as she did. But she was wrong. When Lilian did finally discuss it with others, she found that many felt the same way. She continued to chat about the situation with friends from both school and home, as well as her sister. After many of these conversations, she relates, "something just seemed to change" and her outlook began to improve. Looking back, she admits that even the dreary weather may have had something to do with her flirtation with transferring.

"If, after a semester, you decide you absolutely hate where you are at and feel that you just aren't meant to be there, I say by all means, transfer. It isn't worth your happiness of four years (or more) to stay at a university where you are miserable. However, many students find that after their first month . . . prior negative feelings about the university begin to change."

—Erika Brant, Resident Assistant at
Northern Arizona University,
Class of 2006

Many students who addressed this question offer similar advice: If you're truly, sincerely unhappy with a school, consider transferring—but first make sure you are clear about the reasons why you want to leave.

Kristina Ihlenfeldt (Clemson University, Class of 2003) suggests that some students who live relatively close to their college might be more susceptible to wanting to transfer closer to home. "Is it because you go home every weekend and haven't really given it a chance?" she asks. "If the problem is that you're homesick and/or haven't given it a chance, I would recommend staying, because it's so important to learn how to deal with and adjust to new experiences rather than running away to what is comfortable."

Vinda Rao says she got off to a rocky start at Tufts University, but she pulled through just fine: "The first month of freshman year I wanted to leave 20 times a day. It was a rough time. But once I solidified my friendships, took on leadership positions in my clubs, and got a routine going, I found that I didn't want to go home." By the time winter break rolled around, Vinda, like many college students, realized she was very happy where she was. "I had adjusted to college that completely," she adds, looking back.

For students who've had a rough time adjusting to life at college, it's worth realizing that at least that phase is behind them by the end of the first semester and year. If they go to a new school, they'll have to start that aspect again. On the other hand, if they're not thriving in the college's atmosphere, despite making a sincere effort, transferring may be the right choice.

In her role as a resident assistant at Northern Arizona University, Erika Brant has dealt with lots of students struggling with these issues. She suggests persevering as best as you can through the rough patches. "Even if you don't like something right away—a class, a club, or a roommate—you should at least give it your best try." She urges students to at least do their best to get through a full semester.

7

Thoughts of Home

> *Most people I knew who went home a lot did miss out and also didn't like college as much as the ones who hung around on weekends.*
>
> —Kristina Ihlenfeldt, Clemson University, Class of 2003

The first time students who go away to college refer to their new campus address as "home"—as in, "After I finish at the library, I'm going home"—it can feel sort of strange. In a fleeting moment, they might ask themselves, "Did I really say that?" and just as quickly brush it off with, "Well, I live here, and I kinda like it, so I guess it makes sense."

The experience reflects the dual existence of college students—stepping boldly into a new "home" with one foot while the other remains planted in the doorway of their "real" home, many miles away. Although the adjustment to college is easy for many students, anxiety-inducing dilemmas can surface over situations that were never an issue before: how to stay in contact with parents who are no longer around every day; how to find a way back home and how often to make the trip; and how to adjust to life upon the return to their "real" home, which can suddenly seem like a different place after almost a year away at school.

In some cases, these situations never materialize into worrisome concerns because students adjust smartly, work at their relationships, keep a realistic perspective on things, and also have some good luck. In other cases, students make choices they wish they could reverse in hindsight. This chapter will explore the different ways students have dealt with all sorts of "home life" issues—and provide the benefit of their hindsight.

How often should I return home?

Students on any given dorm floor return to their "real" homes with varying frequencies. Some, especially those attending college on the opposite coast, might only return during semester breaks. Others, especially those who live only a few hours away and have their own car, might head home on most, if not all, weekends. And there are many students in between, who might return once or twice a semester.

No matter how you look at it, a weekend away from campus means fewer opportunities to make social connections in the dorm as well as throughout the college as a whole. For those who return home occasionally, it's not an issue. But those who head home on half the weekends or more could be missing out on some great opportunities.

When she started attending the University of Virginia, Michael Ann Bevivino (Class of 2007) resisted the urge to return regularly to her hometown of Alexandria, about two hours away. Many of her friends from high school, who also attended U.Va., made the trip more routinely. "I didn't go home until our first break, which I think really helped," said Michael Ann. "The students who often went home had a lot of trouble adjusting to life at school. . . . It was hard to not go home at first, but it really helped in the long run because I think that I adjusted more quickly to life away from home."

Denelle Walker used to return home every two weeks to Many, Louisiana, from the Baton Rouge campus of Louisiana State University. "I used the excuse that I needed to do laundry, but in reality, no one drives three-and-a-half hours to wash clothes—I just wanted to be back in familiar surroundings," says Denelle (Class of 2006). "The closer you live, the more tempted you will be to revisit your old stomping grounds."

Then she started to get involved on campus by joining organizations such as student government, participating in study groups, and partaking in campus events. "I had been missing out on all of these things while I was going home," she relates. "By finally participating in all of these things I made friends and began to go home less and less—not because I didn't want to, but because I started to have meetings, and friends started inviting me to go home with them, and I began to call LSU Baton Rouge my home. Now my mom calls me to make sure I am okay, because I only go home on holidays."

> *"I think if I could go back and do my freshman year again, I wouldn't go home that much."*
>
> —Emily Bott, Utah State University, Class of 2006

One sign of a good friendship on campus is a shared anticipation of doing fun things together on the weekends. When the weekends aren't available, neither are the chances for those friendships to form. Jake Liefer (University of Pittsburgh, Class of 2006) observed how this happened with a floormate of his: "My freshman year, there was a guy who lived next to me who never stayed a weekend the whole year because he would go back home to see his girlfriend," he recalls. "The majority of the time the relationships don't last and then they find it difficult to make friends in their sophomore or junior year." By that time, he says, most students already have their core group of friends. It's simply much easier to make friends upon arrival on campus, when everyone's in "make-a-friend" mode.

Jake adds that it's good to visit your parents or sweetheart back at home—but not if those trips become a routine substitute for basic campus relationships. "It is not good to stay attached and be afraid to meet new people," he says.

Once a month is the limit for Ashley Panter, too. Ashley (University of Northern Arizona, Class of 2004) became so immersed in her studies and work that returning home was rarely her first thought. She took occasional visits to her Phoenix home, a little over two hours away from the UNA campus in Flagstaff, usually for special occasions. They were enough to hold any feelings of homesickness at bay. "You'll find that as you get friends and a job, you won't really have time to go home," she says.

Kristina Ihlenfeldt was one of those students who went to school on the other side of the country, and had little choice but to remain

Saving Money When Heading Back Home

Students suggest these ideas for saving cash when traveling back home:

- ✓ Try to catch a ride with a fellow student. Your college might have a matchmaking service whereby you share a ride with a student who has a car and is traveling in the same direction. One possibility: You pay for the gas and tolls, or a meal along the way. That'll still probably be half what you would have to pay to take the bus or train.
- ✓ Take mass transit or shuttle buses to your main mode of transportation, such as the airport or bus depot. Cab rides can comprise a big percentage of your travel budget—you might get a $200 round-trip airfare but then end up spending $50 to $75 more for cabs. You may have to leave a little earlier to make the right connections, but you can save a lot of money. (If a friend is nice enough to drive you, something more than a big "thanks" is in order—maybe a small treat from back home.) Likewise, ask a friend or relative to pick you up and drop you off back at home.
- ✓ Always ask about student rates.
- ✓ Visit some of the many discount Web sites such as CheapTickets.com, Expedia.com, and Priceline.com.
- ✓ Be willing to get bumped from a flight. The inconvenience you face this time around will easily pay for itself next time—when you fly for free.

on campus except for long breaks. Kristina, of Bellingham, Washington, attended Clemson University in South Carolina, graduating in 2003. She only returned home for Christmas break and for the summer each year, but she adapted well to the circumstances. She did observe, though, that there were differences between those who returned home frequently and those who didn't: "During the week, most people are more focused on school, so [those who return home often] won't be around for that time that is devoted almost solely to hanging out with each other."

How often should I e-mail/call my family?

Before they head off to college, students have seen and talked with their parents almost every single day since they can remember. Many times it wasn't even necessary to ask what was going on in each other's lives, because the parents knew when their children were at school, playing soccer, or at a party, and the children knew when Mom and Dad were at work, shopping, or out for the night.

Once students are at college, the change can be strange. Although many get homesick to varying degrees, the situation can be tougher on parents, who are coming to terms with the fact that their child isn't just starting to grow up—she's already there.

Staying in touch, not surprisingly, helps parents and children cope with the immediate picture—what's going on presently in their lives. But regular contact also cultivates what might be considered the bigger picture: the maturation of the parent-child relationship, from one based on paternal nurturing to one grounded in mutual consideration.

"It's the final realization of the process that you are growing up and that you need to become more independent," says Jessica Bal, a student at the University of Connecticut. She calls home every few days, she says, "giving me my space and also helping my mother sever the 'cord' a bit more."

There's no right answer to how often students should stay in touch with their parents. It's a matter of what feels right for both. Jeremy Armstrong (Purdue University, Class of 2007) talks daily if he can work it out, but at least four times a week. Vinda Rao (Tufts

Who Calls Whom?

In most parent-child relationships, it seems that it's the students who decide when the calls will take place. Parents will certainly pick up the phone and call, but most appear to defer to their children's hectic schedules.

Melinda Stiles (University of Minnesota, Twin Cities, Class of 2007) has an arrangement that's common among students. "My parents would sometimes call me at random times," she says. "However, when I set a time each week that I would call, they would respect that and wait for that weekly call."

She tells them about her friends, her classes, and her studies, and knows they appreciate every word. Sometimes, she'll make a surprise call during the week, when they're not expecting to hear from her—and they're always glad to hear each other's voices. She also uses e-mail to send occasional notes. "Parents love hearing about what is going on in your life, and little e-mails will keep them satisfied that you are still alive and well during the week."

University, Class of 2006) calls about twice a week. Once a week seems right for Kris Borer (Carnegie Mellon University, Class of 2006). And while she calls about every three days, Anisa Mohanty (University of North Carolina at Chapel Hill, Class of 2007) knows people who hardly ever call.

"It just depends on what you want," says Emily Bott. "I usually talk to my family about two times a week and let them know what is going on in my life. I usually e-mail at least three times a week to see what my family is doing and how they are all getting along."

Call whenever you want, suggests David Doerkin, a 2004 graduate of Stanford University—just don't think that calling is a sign that you're having trouble settling in at college.

Parents want to hear how classes and activities are going, says Jon Hoggatt of Purdue University, who suggests calling about once a week. "They will greatly appreciate it, and regular communication makes things easier when you come back home next summer."

While e-mail is an efficient way of staying in contact, if you're a regular user of the phone, be sure you're getting a good deal on long-distance rates. Landline phone companies offer reduced rates during the evenings, nights, and weekends. Many cellphone plans allow for unlimited calling late nights (which may be earlier or even later for your folks, depending on the time zone situation). If you're worried about the bill, have your parents call you, or have them call you right back after you first call them. If you don't have a cellphone, see if a friend can loan you hers during the "free" time, suggests Laurel Cooper (Duke University, Class of 2005).

How much should I tell my parents about what really goes on?

No matter how impossible it may seem to believe at times, your parents were once your age. And chances are, they did a lot of the same dumb things you'll likely do during college. If they were to tell you about their past, you might laugh about some of their escapades and wince upon hearing others

It's not too different when you talk to your folks about what's going on in your life today. Students tend to keep a balance when they call home—neither detailing every wild happening nor pretending they're spending every free moment in the library.

Lara Bennett's experiences (University of Scranton, Class of 2006) are characteristic of the balance many students attempt to strike. "Being able to tell them things is a good thing," she says. "I am not saying you need to tell them about the girl or guy you kissed last night, but let them know what's going on in your life. . . . Don't underestimate them—if they went to college, believe me, they know."

Lara says she has an open relationship with her folks—she can tell them anything. While many of her peers don't have that same rapport, she encourages directness in times of trouble: "Honesty is the best key, and if it's something they really need to know, then tell them."

How do you define "times of trouble?" Well, it doesn't only refer to being broke, facing expulsion, or needing a good criminal defense lawyer.

Mela Kirkpatrick (University of North Carolina at Chapel Hill, Class of 2004) says parents aren't just a sounding board—they can offer practical guidance to a son or daughter who's struggling. "It's probably a bad idea to try to hide your unhappiness or difficult situations with friends, professors, or roommates," she says. "They've been there before. They can help."

> *"When I'm down about a long paper or a bad grade, they are the support network that is always there. I frequently relate stories about my friends and classes to my Mom and Dad. They know how it really is, but I usually choose to spare the details that might make them uncomfortable."*
>
> —Tom Brenner, University of Michigan, Class of 2005

Choosing which details to include and which ones to leave out is something that can only be determined individually. Each student knows his parents and how they'll react to different things, says Bill Andrichik (University of Notre Dame, Class of 2007).

He says he keeps in mind the fact that his parents wouldn't approve of everything that happens in school, and he adjusts the level of detail in their conversations accordingly, usually sticking to the basics of academics and extracurricular activities.

Matt Baker (Brigham Young University, Class of 2005) points out that he has a unique perspective on dealing with his parents, because he has lived both at home and at school at different points in his college education. He's seen firsthand how much his parents delight in being part of the experience, and he has been happy to share it with them. "They've enjoyed meeting my friends and roommates and getting to know the girls I've dated," he explains. "In addition, they've been a wonderful source for counsel and support for me as I've decided on a major and struggled with the hardships of college life."

What should I do next summer—and by when should I decide?

Although the academic calendar varies from college to college, the traditional timetable represents a significant scaling back from what most students are used to. Students could be home for the "summer" by the beginning of May—barely halfway through spring. Others might not return home until June, depending on whether their school operates on the semester or trimester system. No matter how your school does it, freshman year will pass quickly.

Despite what some folks might have you believe, the summer from freshman year into sophomore year is not critical. Lots of students spend it sleeping away most of the day, hanging out with their friends, enjoying home cooking, and being lazy. Who can blame them, after being away from home for so long? There's a catch to that "not critical" part, though. It's one thing to not have a formal job. It's another to accomplish absolutely nothing during the summer.

At the very least, the first summer should be a time when students assess their academic experience and performance, move much closer toward selecting a major, and plot to gain practical experience that will be useful when college is over. With at least three months free, summer is the best time to take care of responsibilities that aren't always easy to address once school is in full swing in the fall.

Tom Brenner (University of Michigan at Ann Arbor, Class of 2005) did something different each summer while on break from his studies. After freshman year, he didn't get a paid job—he opted instead to help his dad with projects around their home in Ovid, Michigan. After sophomore year, he worked at a summer camp. Following junior year, he got an internship that helped with his major, aerospace engineering. "I think that these are three pretty typical experiences for a college student during the summer," Tom says. "The most fun was definitely the summer camp job, but I feel like the most important was the internship. In a way though, the most rewarding was the summer that I spent working with my Dad. Don't underestimate how comfortable being at home can be after a year away."

Emily Bott remained at the Logan campus of Utah State University after both her freshman and sophomore years, to work and take classes. She's found it to be a fun experience that helped her meet new friends.

Brian Peterson's experience the summer after his freshman year illustrates the value of planning ahead. Brian (University of Minnesota, Twin Cities, Class of 2007) considered all of the possibilities—taking summer classes, working a summer job back home, or taking one up at school—but instead he chose something out of the ordinary.

"I started thinking a lot about what I wanted during winter break when I had a lot of extra time on my hands and looked at a few options," says Brian. "And by January, I had a good idea of the type of job I wanted to do." He explored summer job opportunities with the National Parks Service, checking out Web sites for information about positions in Yellowstone and Glacier national parks. "I figured that I am only in college once and it is probably the only chance I would have to do something adventuresome and fun."

When he didn't hear back by late March, he looked into opportunities closer to home. He found a lodge on Crane Lake, near the Boundary Waters Canoe Area Wilderness and Voyageur's National Park in northern Minnesota, and applied.

"I gave them a call and it turned out they had some openings—and the next day I was given the job," he recalled in an e-mail from his summer job. "I am currently spending my summer working on the dock staff at Voyagaire Lodge and Houseboats in Crane Lake, Minnesota, and am having a great time with it."

By thinking about the process early in freshman year, Brian had time to conduct research, wait for a response, and then consider alternatives. That's not an easy option for those who wait until March or April to make their first inquiries. And for some high-demand summer jobs, the time to inquire is the fall; some have deadlines as early as December.

When students reflect about their college summers, they rarely speak of how much money they earned, or didn't. Instead, they focus on the experience—how it enriched their life, broadened their mindset, or was just plain fun. It doesn't matter much if the results were achieved working in a lodge, going to class, visiting another country (even for just a vacation), or volunteering somewhere.

Preplan Your Way to an Exciting Summer

A desire to try new things often leads to great things. Minal Ahson (University of Miami, Class of 2005) spent the summer before her junior year in Tanzania, researching healthcare issues and the HIV/AIDS crisis in the east African country. Her journey was funded by the Patrick Stewart Human Rights Scholarship, administered through Amnesty International. "It was an amazing experience that I am extremely grateful to have had," Minal says. "This took a bit of planning and research to figure out the logistics, write my proposal, apply for the award, etc. I found it useful to use winter and spring breaks to figure this out, since classes and exams are not going on."

Of course, money is a real concern for most students. But money—coming up with it, or earning it—shouldn't exclude you from having enriching summer experiences. It's possible to volunteer on a part-time basis while working a paid job, or to secure a summer scholarship, or to find a job that will also cover room or board for the summer. What's needed is the foresight to plan ahead, the determination to make a connection, and the drive to make a difference in your life—and maybe in others' lives as well.

How will I adjust to life at home next summer?

If adjusting to life at college was a challenge, then readjusting to life at home the following summer can be . . . well, it can be an even bigger challenge.

After eight or nine months of setting your own hours, doing as you please, sleeping until 2 in the afternoon at times, and eating whatever and whenever you want—to name some freedoms—any limits set by Mom and Dad can come across as hopelessly inflexible and unwarranted.

Even the most reasonable requests from the folks (like "Could you at least call us if you're not coming home tonight?") can seem burdensome.

Some students figure out what's going on their first weekend home in May or June; for others, it takes a summer of bickering and snapping at Mom and Dad before they come to this realization: It's their house—they set the rules.

David Doerkin says compromise is involved, and students' best strategy is to show they understand there are rules. "It might be hard to readjust to your parents' rules, but it is their house and you have the choice of not coming back home," he says. "Respect your parents and they will respect you."

When students demonstrate such empathy, they frequently notice that Mom and Dad show some surprising new flexibility. As parents sense their sons' and daughers' maturation, it's easier for them to view their children as different individuals than the ones who wrapped up high school just a year ago. It dawns on them that the old high-school limits don't entirely apply anymore.

But don't be mistaken—there are still limits. Moms and dads will never adjust to their children returning home at 4 in the morning. Never. It's not that they don't trust their sons and daughters; it's that they don't trust anything or anybody at that hour. The only thing they trust is their son or daughter, at home, in bed. Asleep.

Anisa Mohanty tries to understand why parents might get concerned about situations such as late hours. While such thinking helps, she has still been exasperated at the abrupt changes to her lifestyle: "I'm still trying to figure this out," she explained early in her first summer home from UNC. "Curfews are difficult . . . once you've been to college, it's very difficult to tolerate."

Rebecca Wood (University of Memphis, Class of 2005) also endured a rough transition from "complete freedom back to parental control." She felt like she went from living like an adult to living like a child. But she says she learned that it's better to work with her parents than against them.

"The best thing for me was to make my parents feel included," she says. She let them meet her friends, and provided reassurance by telling them what she was doing and when. She didn't go into every single detail, but she found out that they didn't ask for every detail. By taking the initiative to communicate with her folks, she headed off the who-what-when-where line of questioning that always leads to anguish.

> *"It's difficult to justify why you want to be out until 1 or 2 a.m., especially on a weeknight. It's hard to explain that in college, things get started at 11 p.m. It's also difficult because parents will still be parents . . . [however] they do eventually loosen up to the idea of you taking road trips and vacations alone and things of that nature."*
>
> —Anisa Mohanty, University of North Carolina at Chapel Hill, Class of 2007

Despite some of the concerns you might face upon returning home, don't forget that there are some aspects of home life that are indisputably welcome.

Tom Brenner spent 10 hours a day in bed his first summer back home, thoroughly enjoying the home cooking, and appreciating the break from doing his own laundry. "I found it fairly easy to adjust to being back home," he says.

And Vinda Rao was glad for one minor change in her daily routine: "Showering without wearing sandals is all the justification I need to stay home," she says.

8

Sleep

> *It's the worst thing when you don't get enough sleep. The alarm is five times as loud as you thought it was, you swear you just went to sleep 10 minutes ago, your eyes are screaming as you desperately try to put your contacts in, and somehow, you're running late. You just have to get up and go.*
>
> —Debra Trevino, University of Texas at Austin, Class of 2005

With so much happening just about every minute of the day, it's no wonder that college students find it easiest to cut back on sleep when the alternative is cutting back on schoolwork or socializing.

It's an easy, and usually harmless, choice if it's done once in a while. But persistent neglect of sleep can adversely affect students' lives—they may skip early classes, not pay attention or fall asleep in class, take long afternoon naps, or sleep in until 2 p.m. on Saturdays and Sundays. The result is a constant cycle of catch-up that can only be broken by getting sufficient sleep every night in the first place.

In a response that may not solve the problem, but may help alleviate some symptoms, Duke University has made it easy to avoid classes that start at 8 a.m.—by eliminating them. Starting in the fall of 2004, no classes start before 8:30 in the morning. The reason: Students avoided the 8 a.m. classes so much that the university was forced to reconsider its scheduling patterns.

Duke's students were getting too little sleep to benefit from class, according to university officials. "They begin to get into a pattern of sleeping four to five hours," James Clack, Duke's director of counseling and psychological services, told The Associated Press. "They really think it doesn't bother them, but that really isn't the case."

This chapter will explore students' sleep patterns—how they make sure they get enough rest to be alert in class, how they catch up on sleep when they need to, and how they manage when sleep takes a back seat to other priorities.

What time should I go to sleep?

You might have a sleep plan when you arrive at college, even if it's something you've only given a moment's thought to. And while it's possible that you'll stick to the hours you envisioned, it's more likely you'll need to adjust to what's going on in your life. What's your workload like? When do your classes start? What are the hours of your part-time job? How much sleep do you need? What are your commitments to extracurricular clubs and groups? What's your roommate like? How much will you be hanging out with your floormates?

The answers will dictate whether your lights go out at 11 p.m., midnight, 1 a.m., or later.

John Andersen's first semester at the University of Missouri–Columbia involved major adjustments to his personal routine, including his sleep habits. Although he got along well with his roommate, John had to get used to the fact that their different schedules sometimes meant he'd get disturbed while sleeping. "He was rushing a fraternity," says John, a member of the class of 2007. "Anyone who had a roommate do this knows exactly what I am talking about. He was never around when I decided to go to bed and then usually around 2 or 3 a.m. he would finally get into the room. He would sneak in, trying to be as quiet as possible so I would not wake up. However, I usually did."

John took it in stride: The two would usually chat for a few minutes and then John would get back to sleep. "I really didn't mind too much because I knew that we were two different people and that we had different activities we were each involved in."

Adam Ritton (Creighton University, Class of 2007) also learned to adjust. When he arrived for freshman year at the campus in Omaha, Nebraska, he planned to follow his high-school schedule—going to bed at 10 p.m. and waking up at 6:30 a.m.

"That didn't last past the first day," says Adam. "It was so hard to go to bed because there was always something going on every night that I wanted to participate in. I finally set a time of midnight to go to bed and luckily, my roommate complied."

Jamie Veasey (Evansville University, Class of 2006) experienced a similar schedule shift: In high school, she'd go to bed between 9 and 11 p.m., but not in college. "Some nights I may be working on a paper and not get to bed until 4 in the morning," she says. "Most nights I go to bed around 2 a.m."

Of course, there's room to study, socialize, and get to bed at a reasonable hour. It just takes some planning and determination to do all three.

Dorm Life, Late p.m./Early a.m.

You'll not be alone on your floor if you're still awake in the middle of the night. Some students quietly study or write papers in the late, late hours, while others watch TV or join in chatfests, both virtual and in-person. It's all an extension of the relaxed pace that pervades dorms in the post-dinner hours. Sure, there's plenty of studying going on in the evening and late at night, but it's easy to find someone taking a break, or willing to take one (as in, "Wanna hit the snack bar?" "I'm in."). It's also a time when students listen to music, surf the Web, watch TV or movies, and just hang out. That atmosphere may make it tough to get started on your schoolwork, or to get back to it, according to Catherine Bell (University of Kansas, Class of 2004): "A great college experience will be filled with late-night talks with your new friends, cramming for a test the next day, and student activities that take up your afternoons and force you to study late at night," she says.

Erick M. Bousman (University of South Carolina, Class of 2006) has no trouble going to bed earlier than most students. "If my day is active enough, it is rather easy to make sure that by 11 p.m. or so I am dead tired enough to want to go to sleep," he says. Holly Woodhead (Gettysburg College, Class of 2005) also goes to bed "early"—at 11 p.m.—and wakes up at 7 in the morning. She admits she sometimes gets teased about her hours, but she doesn't mind, because she knows she'll be alert instead of groggy for her early classes. "Most people are not like I am and like to go to bed late and wake up late," says Holly. "If you are not a morning person . . . don't sign up for classes at 9 a.m. because chances are you will be that person nodding off in the back of the room."

How will I make sure I get enough sleep?

For busy students, planning a sleep schedule can seem as challenging as planning a class schedule. Sleep, like schoolwork, can be easy to neglect—especially in an environment where socializing opportunities exist just about 24 hours a day. To extend the parallel: Those who neglect sleep, just like those who neglect their schoolwork, usually end up wishing they found the time.

The right amount of sleep varies among students, most of whom aren't like Erica Lemansky (Brandeis University, Class of 2005). Erica is able get by on less sleep than many of her peers during the school week. On weekends, she sleeps until later in the morning or naps during the day.

Three or four hours a night was the rule for Jessica Martin (Western Kentucky University, Class of 2005) for the year and a half that she served as a resident adviser. On most nights, she was either studying or spending some time with the residents on her floor. Sleep was always pushed to the background. Although she got used to the routine, she knew it wasn't the best thing for her. "It wasn't healthy and I don't advise it," says Jessica.

> *"I'm one of those four-to-five-hours-a-night, multiple-cups-of-coffee girls who, with some caffeine and a nice hot shower, can be up and at work at 7:45 a.m. after finishing up a paper at 2 a.m."*
>
> —Erica Lemansky, Brandeis University, Class of 2005

On the other hand, Debra Trevino (University of Texas at Austin, Class of 2005) realizes she needs eight hours of sleep each night, "or I'm grumpy." And since she also likes to stay up late at night, she schedules her classes to start in the late morning or early afternoon. On the days where she knows she has to get up early, she makes sure she goes to bed early.

Debra's routine works for her—that's what matters most—but it may not work for others.

Ginger Ruskamp (Creighton University, Class of 2005) followed a similar pattern, but then realized it wasn't the best strategy for her: "I found that when my classes started later in the day, I usually slept all morning. And when I did wake up I felt like I had already wasted half of my day." She found that classes that start at 9:30 or 10:30 a.m. work best because they give her time to sleep in a little, but still allow for a productive morning.

She also realized that a convenient time slot shouldn't be the sole reason for choosing a class. She learned this when she faced a choice about a required course for her degree: take the 8:30 a.m. class with a professor she heard great things about, or take the 11 a.m. class with an unknown professor. She opted for the 11 a.m. class.

Do you even need to hear the rest of the story?

"I didn't really learn anything in the class and earned only a B," Ginger recalls. "If I had just taken the 8:30 class, I would have learned the material better and probably would have gotten an A. That grade on my transcript is a permanent reminder that the teacher is a better indicator of a class than the time of day."

For the many students who have trouble waking up at any time, Erica Lemansky suggests scheduling something you're especially interested in—such as a class you particularly want to take, or a workout at the gym. This provides an incentive to get out of bed and makes it a little less likely that you'll dread the first few hours of the day, she adds.

But consistency is more important than a set bedtime or wake-up time. Sleeping until noon some days and getting up at 8 a.m. other days is sure to keep one's sleep patterns off balance, as Jake Liefer (University of Pittsburgh, Class of 2006) discovered. One semester he started class at 10 a.m. two days a week, while the other days he didn't have to start until 1 p.m. "It didn't work out all that well," he says. The uneven schedule made it difficult to get into a groove, and he's sought a more consistent schedule in subsequent semesters.

Good Sleep Habits

The following sleep habits are recommended by experts:

- ✓ Give yourself an honest assessment of how much sleep you need each night, and work your schedule around that. For example, if you absolutely need eight hours of sleep, but must be awake by 8 a.m., you should plan to be in bed by midnight.
- ✓ If you usually wake up at 8 or 9 a.m., resist the temptation to sleep in until noon on days off. Although sleeping an extra hour is fine on the weekends, for example, sleeping three or four extra hours will throw off your internal sleep rhythms and ultimately make it tougher to wake up on school days.
- ✓ Avoid big meals before bedtime–you'll sleep better.
- ✓ See your doctor if you have trouble falling asleep, if you wake up frequently during the night, or have any other problem that may be related to your sleep routine.

Are naps a good idea?

Students who never napped before college might find them hard to resist once they get settled in their routines—especially if the routines include challenging classes, late nights, and early mornings. A student might return to her dorm room after lunch—say around 2 p.m.—put on some music, sit on the bed briefly, decide to lie down for a moment to stretch, realize that she only had six hours of sleep last night, and then figure she's entitled to an extra hour or so of shut-eye.

She'll fall into a deep sleep, and wake to the sounds of her floormates talking in the hallway . . . about . . . going to dinner.

Yes, dinner. Time can sail by when you're comfortable and undisturbed because your roommate's in biology lab for the afternoon. As a result, 2 p.m. can quickly turn into 5 p.m.

Samuel Bair (University of Alaska Anchorage, Class of 2005) likes his naps, but to avoid drifting asleep for the afternoon or early evening, he sets his alarm clock.

To Nap or Not to Nap

Many students do not feel refreshed after their extended siestas. "I can't nap," says Debra Trevino. "All of my friends say that they'll just take a nap to make up for missing sleep. I just can't do it. When I try to, I usually nap for about three hours, wake up disoriented, groggy, and even more tired than before I napped. Plus, you get those weird fast dreams whenever you nap that are very confusing and strange . . . naps just throw everything off."

Catherine Anne Bennion (Brigham Young University, Class of 2007) agrees that naps disturb her regular sleep cycle. As a result, she only snoozes when she absolutely has to, like the day after she's pulled an all-nighter.

Students who do nap regularly say their secret is not relying on them too heavily and generally limiting them to an hour or less.

Places to Grab a Quick Nap

Your dorm room, by the way, isn't the only place to take a short rest. Using your backpack as a pillow, you can briefly doze off anywhere you can put your head down:

- ✓ Cody Quintero sometimes lies on the grass on the main campus at the University of Kansas.
- ✓ Jessica Martin of Western Kentucky University will nap on the couch in the Student Government Association office.
- ✓ Erick M. Bousman of the University of South Carolina catches a few winks in the field near his dorm.
- ✓ Other favorite spots for students include the library and student lounges.

That works well—unless, like Holly Woodhead has done, you smack the snooze bar into submission: "Without realizing it, you have slept until 7 and still have work to finish for the next day," she says, reflecting on her own experiences.

Holly, for example, likes to take half-hour naps around 4 in the afternoon. "You will feel refreshed and ready for a long night of work," she says, although she cautions about a down side. "Four p.m. is the prime time for students to gather outside of residence halls and play soccer, Wiffle ball, or lacrosse. As a result, I often found that I would skip the nap and spend time with my friends."

While it's best for most students to get seven to nine hours of sleep each night, as noted earlier, it's not always possible, and short naps might be a necessity, not a luxury: You might occasionally work at your campus job until 11 p.m., for example, and then, at one point, have to finish an assignment until 2 a.m. With a class at 8:30 the next morning, you can expect a modest "sleep deficit" to build.

As a result, students say that short power naps help get them through the day.

Cody Quintero (University of Kansas, Class of 2007) says brief naps reduce stress: "There are just times when you need that alone time to yourself, and even a 30-minute nap to get you reenergized makes the biggest difference," says Cody. "You can't keep your mind burning all day—it needs a break, too, in order for you to have mental wellness."

"I love naps because they can give you an extra boost of energy to finish out the day," says Ginger Ruskamp. "And sometimes when you are working on something and are very tired, it is better to take a short nap and wake up refreshed and ready to work. But excessive napping is not a good idea. It is better for your body to get into a regular sleep pattern. And this will help you have more energy in your classes to begin with."

> *"You have to make time for yourself. And if sleep is what you need, do it. There will come a time when being with your friends isn't nearly as important as getting some long-awaited rest."*
>
> —Jessica Martin, Western Kentucky University, Class of 2005

Should I pull an all-nighter?

Jake Liefer likes the pressure of last-minute work. When faced with a deadline, he often becomes a highly capable academic machine, cranking out quality material that earns him good grades.

It's a strategy many students swear by, and when the grades back up their efforts, it's tough to argue with them. But any student's reliance on last-minute efficiency faces its toughest test when the assignments are huge—such as a semester-long project or a 12-page paper.

The "last-minute," in these cases, can often extend to a grueling all-night, high-stress affair. Sometime around 1 or 2 a.m., the realization sets in that it's going to be a very late night, and that maybe some coffee or a few cans of Coke are in order.

The Infamous All-Nighter

For most students, as long as work continues to be due at the start of class, the all-nighter remains an option. All-nighters hold legendary status on campus. Everyone has a story about them. To some, completing an all-nighter is a badge of honor—the ultimate sign of their will to succeed. Others see them as the ultimate, pathetic sign that they couldn't get their act together until confronted with the possibility of failing.

"Students tend to brag about how many all-nighters they have pulled, but these make them moody and edgy," says Jessica Martin. "I have only pulled two and the day after each I felt horrible."

It would be one thing if that horrible feeling—a body too tired to move, a brain too tapped to think—was the only price to pay for putting in a top-notch performance on an academic endeavor, but sometimes additional pain awaits.

"Once I stayed up until 4 a.m. studying for a final, and I ended up sleeping through my final," remembers Cody Quintero. And many students discover, when they get their grades back, that they really don't do their best work at the last minute.

An all-nighter is on the horizon, and rare is the student who can handle one unscathed.

"By the time 4 or 5 a.m. rolls around, you're like "Why can't I do this?" says Jake. "You end up staring at a computer screen for 30 minutes, trying to find the answer to a problem. You're a walking zombie."

Jake pulled all-nighters three or four times in the spring of his sophomore year and regrets it. "You think, 'If I would have started an hour or two earlier. . . .'" Of course, it's even better to start a day or two earlier—or a week or two earlier.

Jake found some relief in one class, in which a professor set a midnight deadline for assignments. The strategy worked well—students who waited until the last minute at least finished their work at a reasonable time.

With a paper due every Friday during her first semester at Yale University, Yassmin Sadeghi (Class of 2007) ended up regularly pulling all-nighters. It didn't take her long to realize that she had to find a better way. By the time spring semester rolled around, she took control of her academics, cut down on procrastinating, and improved her time management. "The papers I wrote pulling all-nighters were really not works I was too proud of," says Yassmin. "And I always felt I could have done a much better job had I written the paper or studied for the test during the day, as opposed to at 5 a.m., while I was nodding off.

"If you have a manageable amount of work and you set aside time to do it during the day, you should not have to pull an all-nighter . . . but if worst comes to worst, grab several cups of coffee and get to work."

Grace Choe recalls pulling a few all-nighters—and getting good grades in those classes—in high school, when the work load was no doubt lighter. It's been a different story in college: "Ever since I came to SC, I am a wreck when I do an all-nighter," she says. In the spring of her junior year, she says she pulled about three of them, each time because she had procrastinated. "Not surprisingly, I got a really bad grade on those projects, but for the tests that I split up into three days [of studying], doing semi-all-nighters, I got a much better grade."

Adam Ritton recalls going into the final exam in a course on the modern Western world with a solid B. But he wanted a B+. He pushed himself through an all-nighter to get the higher grade . . . and succeeded. But then he had four more finals to take.

"I was so tired and worn out from all that studying that I winged the next four exams without so much as looking at my books," he recalls. "Will I ever pull an all-nighter again? Probably, but I hope not, because they kill."

For those deciding whether to stay up all night, there is a middle ground that can be taken occasionally: Study hard, late into the night—say until 2 or 3 a.m.—then get maybe four of five hours of sleep, followed by an early-morning study session.

Try a Practice All-Nighter Before Pulling a Real One

Meredith Schweitzer (Vanderbilt University, Class of 2006) didn't wait until the last minute for her first all-nighter. In fact, she took hers without the pressure of a midterm or a paper due the next day. She and her friends pulled a "practice all-nighter" their freshman year just to experience it. It convinced her that all-nighters should be a last resort, especially if they involve studying for a test. "It was fun at the time—hanging out with friends all night and going to breakfast the next day," Meredith says. "But, honestly, chugging Coke all night to get enough caffeine in order to stay awake doesn't really put you in a great state of mind to study information and retain it later—it just makes you tired."

Others suggest looking at the big picture: How much is it worth it to get a slightly higher grade—especially if it means you might sleepwalk through the rest of your classes the following day?

Students disagree on the merits of going to class in that zombielike state. While some professors may appreciate a student's effort to show up during high-stress midterm weeks, others might prefer an apologetic e-mail explaining the unique circumstances while the student catches up on desperately needed rest.

Kristen Watts of the University of Texas at Austin (Class of 2006) takes a more pragmatic approach to all-nighters. She's aware that some students swear by them while others swear at them. Her strategy? They're no big deal, as long as the rest of your life is in order. "I've come to realize that balance is the name of the game," she says. "So long as you generally have a balanced lifestyle of ample doses of sleep, regular exercise, and a healthy diet, then once in a while, the infamous all-nighter will not do you in," she says. That's not to say that she highly recommends them: "Do realize that the next day when you're rambling senselessly to your professor as you hand in that paper, you may not sound so intelligible, and you may not feel so hot."

9

Campus Life

> ***I find it uncanny how just joining a single club can make your college experience so much more rich and fulfilling, and would recommend it to any college student.***
>
> —Holly Jericoff, University of Idaho, Class of 2005

Have you found a "comfort zone"—your favorite people and activities—that contains everything you want?

Great. Now abandon it.

Doing so is a common thread among students who've squeezed each drop from their college experience as if it was liquid gold. They've maximized every moment by fearlessly pursuing their interests, meeting new people, and trying different activities. By going outside their comfort zone, they discover themselves.

Some students go rock climbing, while some build homes for homeless families. Some run for student government, while others take their studies to the other side of the world.

Exhilarating experiences like those are the payoff for bypassing the safest, most traveled path in favor of taking a risk to try something fresh. The reward might also include the sense of satisfaction that only comes from making a difference or helping the less fortunate.

Jarita Lindsey (St. Louis University, Class of 2007) is an example. Even though she always enjoyed volunteering, she at first thought joining a formal service fraternity like Alpha Phi Omega would be "a bit out of my comfort zone." But Jarita is glad she took the time to check it out. Her volunteer endeavors have included helping Girl Scouts serve at a homeless shelter and tutoring students in need. "I think that if I hadn't joined APO then I would have probably joined a group within my comfort zone and probably would have prevented myself from the character growth I have experienced," she says.

This stuff doesn't happen for those who don't take chances and don't push themselves to their limits. It's what advisers mean when they say "grades aren't everything." In fact, those three words should be stamped on every diploma, because a college degree only demonstrates how a student handled one aspect of college life. The graduate who soaked up all that her school had to offer and received mostly B's, for example, is better rounded than the one who received straight A's but never ventured far from the dorm room or classroom.

This chapter explores how students have gotten involved in campus activities, clubs, and groups, how they make the most out of their time, and how they match their interests with what's available on campus.

How do I handle all this free time?

When Melissa Hernandez (Colby College, Class of 2005) plotted her freshman-year schedule, she was amazed at the number of empty blocks, giving the illusion of a bounty of free time: "I remember walking into college thinking, 'Sweet, only four classes!'" recalls Melissa. But once she started working a part-time job, writing English papers, volunteering, and otherwise getting involved on campus, she had few extra moments to herself.

Her experience is common among first-year students. A certain shock can set in when they realize that they'll be in class about half as much as in high school. And with few assignments usually due the first weeks of class, it can seem like there's almost too much free time. Those who pack their schedules with activities and opportunities find themselves quickly engrossed and rarely complaining that they have little time to sit around.

During her freshman year, for example, Yassmin Sadeghi (Yale University, Class of 2007) joined the Freshman Class Council and the Yale Political Union, and participated in community-service projects. "In retrospect, I'm really glad I got so involved my first semester because it allowed me to meet a lot of people and discover what I was most interested in," says Yassmin.

> *"Free time? What free time? I work two jobs and take classes. I am busy every moment of the day. My only down time comes on weekends [when] I . . . catch up on homework. Staying busy keeps you out of trouble."*
>
> —Aaron Turner, Bowling Green State University, Class of 2005

Like many students, Grace Choe (University of Southern California, Class of 2005) finds she's much better off when she's busy. "There are so many awesome opportunities here, one would be a fool to pass on them," she says. "I'm constantly active and I don't have time to slack off. If I have free time during the day . . . I tend to get into a vegetative state. The worst semester I had was when I was taking only three classes and had one campus activity. I got two C's and a B. These were easy classes!"

It may seem unusual to hear Grace explain why she needs to keep busy to do her best in school. But it's an assertion successful students repeatedly cite. Some further explanation might help.

Students who are intensely involved typically work hard to manage their schedules to fit everything in—with time set aside for academics, part-time jobs, and clubs. They like to hang out, go out, watch TV, and talk on the phone like all students, but for them such activities are a lower priority. Those with excessive free time often approach the situation from the other side: They spend so much time hanging out, watching TV, and socializing that they struggle to find room for academics.

By the way, no one suggests that an occasional lazy day, or a little lazy time every day, is a problem. Sometimes it's good to devote a few hours to reality TV, hacky-sack, or PlayStation 2. The idea is that if you skip class or delay term-paper research to catch the latest episode of "General Hospital" or "Survivor: Cleveland," you might need to rearrange your priorities.

Why should I get involved with campus organizations?

Extracurricular activities—campus clubs and groups—may be the most overlooked indicator of a college or university's quality. Why? Students who get involved may spend more time in those activities than they do in class. And those activities may help them succeed in life as much as their diploma.

A journalism major who edits her school newspaper leaves college ready to work at a "real" paper, because the difference is minimal in many ways. A student who organizes a charity dance marathon has valuable event-management skills in addition to a bachelor's degree. A member of the debate team possesses the invaluable talent of articulating his thoughts clearly and persuasively. Even the president of the hacky-sack club has flexed some leadership muscle in college.

You may not have checked out every extracurricular activity on campus before arriving at school, but your employers notice when you've used those activities to improve yourself.

Grace Choe, who in the previous section explained her passion for getting involved, is a public relations major at the University of Southern California. It was only natural for her to join USC's chapter of the Public Relations Student Society of America. "I've met so many P.R. professionals from many of the top agencies in L.A. and have learned a lot about the industry," says Grace, who has served as secretary of the group. "I've kept in contact with several of them and I do bump into them during P.R. events. This is a great head start in an industry that I am going to pursue and it shows these professionals—since they see me often—that I am serious about my future."

Grace hopes to follow in the footsteps of a friend of hers who was president of her school's accounting club. The friend ended up being recruited by top accounting firms before she graduated because she had networked so successfully at club-related events.

As a dual major in business marketing and communications, Cody Quintero's involvement with the Association of University Residence Halls at the University of Kansas has been both rewarding and enriching. "I have had the opportunity to attend national conferences and represent my school in ways that I never thought possible," says Cody (Class of 2007). "I have been able to plan events that affected almost 1,000 students. . . . There are things that I can put on my resume that I would have never been able to if I did not get involved."

The difference between high-school extracurricular activities and those in college, Cody points out, is that the students handle every single responsibility in college clubs, providing practical experience. "Joining campus clubs always gives you opportunities that you will never experience anywhere else," he adds.

Students just don't join clubs to advance their career opportunities. They join to explore their social interests, meet new people, and have fun. What follows can often have a broader impact on your college career and even your life.

Be Willing to Take the First Step

"You'll have to do some work to find a group that's right for you," says John Andersen (University of Missouri–Columbia, Class of 2007). "They will not come and get you. You have to be proactive. If you don't seek the opportunities yourself, you will never find them."

John had no idea what groups he'd join when he showed up on the Missouri campus, so he attended a fair to learn more about his options. "There is literally something for everyone," he says. "I had never even given thought to joining student government until I saw our student government table and asked what I would have to do to get involved. They told me to come to the meeting that night and give a one-minute speech on why I would make a good student senator. It turned out that I never even had to speak because we had less people than open seats, so all I did was come to one meeting and I was officially a senator."

Elizabeth Flynn (University of Tennessee, Knoxville, Class of 2004) got involved with the annual Dance Marathon during her freshman year simply because she was "looking for things to do." It seemed like a worthwhile endeavor, and several of her friends had joined up, as well. The event raises funds for East Tennessee Children's Hospital's hematology and oncology unit.

Her interest blossomed into a commitment that spanned her four years at Tennessee, allowing her to give to a highly worthy cause while also having fun and building her career credentials. In her sophomore year, Elizabeth was appointed to the executive committee and oversaw the event's catering. In her junior and senior years, she handled public relations—her field of study.

"I took what I was interested in doing as a career and put my skills to work in both these positions," says Elizabeth. "I was able to learn a lot about fundraising, event planning, and crowd control during my time as director of catering, and I developed a media kit, got articles placed in the campus newspaper, and served as a liaison to the media as director of media relations."

Similarly, Jake Liefer (University of Pittsburgh, Class of 2006) gained interpersonal skills as president of the Resident Student Association, a group he initially joined because it was the first thing that jumped out at him and because the meeting was held in his dorm. "It helps with interacting—dealing with people, dealing with situations," says Jake. "You get outside your comfort zone."

Those skills helped when he was named publicity chair for his fraternity, Lambda Chi Alpha, which was hosting a teeter-totter marathon to raise funds for the Big Brother Big Sister organization. While Jake had no formal training in the field, he managed to send out press releases and generate interest among the Pittsburgh media. Eventually, he grew comfortable fielding inquiries and speaking to the press because of his experience with the Resident Student Association.

How will I manage my time if I'm involved in activities on campus?

With coursework in magazine journalism, women's studies, and political science, as well as a full slate of campus activities, Jean

Stevens (Syracuse University, Class of 2006) must coordinate her schedule carefully to succeed. Jean takes a consistent approach each semester: It starts by spending the first few days getting acclimated to the new routine and sizing up the challenges ahead. After figuring out what she can handle, she digs into her activities, among them the Honors Student Association, the Student Environmental Action Coalition, and the University 100, a group of student ambassadors. She's also a reporter for the *Daily Orange* student newspaper.

When the semester is in full swing, Jean balances her interests and academics by employing time-management skills. She maintains a planner and uses it regularly, confessing that she'd be lost without it. She wakes up early enough to get everything organized for the day. And she wastes no time. For example, she places phone calls for *Daily Orange* articles either before she heads out for class or during her class breaks.

"In class, I pay attention 120 percent, because I've learned that knowing what goes on in class and taking careful notes makes the difference between an A or B, and you won't need to take as much extra time to study for exams," she says.

Lastly, she prioritizes everything; she rarely watches TV because she knows it would be at the expense of something more important on her schedule. "It's really about seeing the big picture, and knowing what can be done, when," she says.

Success with juggling activities and academics also involves taking on no more than you can handle, to avoid overextending yourself. For example, as heavily involved as she was freshman year, Yassmin Sadeghi of Yale University says it might have been better if she scaled back a bit. "I often felt like I was doing a million things first semester," she says.

Students who get over-involved might suffer academically, and won't even get the full benefit of the clubs because they're spreading themselves too thin, says Catherine Bell (University of Kansas, Class of 2004). "You won't make a positive difference in the organization if you are running to the next event."

> *"Don't go out and join every club on campus. Choose a few that fit your interests and that you are willing to commit your time to. I am involved in several different campus clubs and I am currently, or have been, actively involved in every one. There are other clubs that I would like to join, but I don't, because I know that I do not have the time to fully commit to them."*
>
> —Ginger Ruskamp, Creighton University, Class of 2005

How do I find a club or group that's right for me?

Whether you join one campus group or a half dozen, make sure that your time is well spent. Students follow a number of strategies when searching for campus organizations:

- ✓ They find out what's available. It's impossible to know about every group on campus—and likely that you'll miss some great opportunities—unless you try to learn about them by visiting campus Web sites or attending activity fairs, for example.
- ✓ They sample groups' meetings or activities to see if they match up with the people or the programming.
- ✓ They ask questions to find out how others enjoy the group, and to learn what the time and financial commitment will be.

"What do you care about? What do you love to do?" Those are two questions Kristen Watts (University of Texas at Austin, Class of 2006) suggests students keep in mind when choosing from the menu of extracurricular offerings. "At your school's freshman orientation, you'll probably be bombarded with information on this club and that. Take all the fliers and maybe give a few of the clubs your e-mail address."

Although a group's goals and activities will attract interest initially, the fellow members are the real reason you'll stick with a club or organization, says Kristen, who is president of her cluster of dorms, a member of the Fellowship of Christian Athletes, and a member of the university's rowing team. "These people are teaching me more than I could learn in class; they're becoming my friends for life."

Students say it's essential to at least try an activity if you're not sure about it. If it's not what you had in mind, you don't have to go back. And of course, if you enjoy it, it was well worth checking out in the first place.

But you'll never know unless you try.

Bethany Sheldon (Boston University, Class of 2006) was a cheerleader in high school, and initially did not plan to try out at BU. But curiosity got the best of her. "I ended up going to the tryouts just to see what it was like," she says.

She made the team—and is glad she decided to check out the opportunity, because it has enriched her college experience. "Cheerleading has been one of the biggest highlights of my college career so far," she says. "I met my two best friends at college through cheering."

Julia Bauler (Gonzaga University, Class of 2005) agrees with the open-minded approach. "Interests change over time," she says, and students are free to try new things. At the same time, joining a group may lead to unexpected benefits. For example, Julia was active in Gonzaga's chapter of the Residence Hall Association, and has served as executive vice president. That led to a campus job in the university's housing department. "Opportunities and activities always lead to other adventures," she says.

It may not be easy to find a club that's the right fit for you. If that's the case, don't get discouraged, says Holly Jericoff. Instead, network—talk to fellow students, professors, and advisers. Holly found a great deal of support from the Idaho faculty; one professor even offered to help her launch a group and serve as adviser.

Some students might be intimidated by the array of clubs to join, or feel—perhaps correctly—that their views differ from those held by the majority of students.

> *"Don't get frustrated. I tried many groups and clubs out before I really found one that I was genuinely interested and passionate about."*
>
> —Holly Jericoff, University of Idaho, Class of 2005

Adam Abelkop (Wake Forest University, Class of 2007) found himself in the latter situation: "Even at Wake Forest—a more conservative campus—I've found it easy to participate and distinguish myself in the liberal clubs," says Adam, who is president of the College Democrats. He contrasts his situation to that of like-minded students at larger, more liberal campuses, where it might be easier to blend in, but possibly tougher to stand out.

When trying to connect with clubs, Adam suggests taking inventory of what you do in your spare time. "Chances are that there is a club for it, and if not, then it's not at all hard to start a new club."

That's what Debra Trevino (Class of 2005) did at the University of Texas at Austin, where she founded two student organizations: "I started A.M.I.G.O.S. (Active Minds Integrating Goals, Opportunity, and Spirit) because I wanted a social group that was comprised of true friends and nonjudgmental membership," says Debra. "I just formed Texas S.T.A.R.S. (Students Taking Active Roles in Society) . . . as a way to get students to volunteer in their community."

Ironically, Debra arrived at Texas after engaging in more than her share of leadership activities in high school and even middle school. At first, she planned to stay in the background, but that just wasn't her style. "I realized I couldn't just sit back and not be involved with my campus," she says. "Even with small, new groups like A.M.I.G.O.S. and S.T.A.R.S., I felt I have already contributed to the university."

A.M.I.G.O.S. started with a burst of inspiration from Debra to her roommates. They were supportive, Debra recalls, but she got the impression that they didn't think she'd go through with establishing a new group. The university made it easy to do so. The Campus & Community Involvement division helped with the paperwork and provided facilities and guidance needed to launch the group—not to mention plenty of encouragement. Within months, the group counted 25 members. In part because setting up A.M.I.G.O.S. was so easy, Debra was motivated to establish S.T.A.R.S.

If you have an idea, share it with others, as Debra Trevino did at Texas. It's the only way to see if your idea can germinate.

Irene Fernando, Nick Lindberg, Brian Peterson, and Greg Tehven were freshmen at the University of Minnesota, Twin Cities, who had shared interests and wanted to get involved. Greg had spent the previous summer volunteering at the National Leadership Camp in Australia, where he heard about "Pay It Forward" tours—in which volunteers take road trips and perform acts of good will in cities along the way.

"Greg shared this idea with us soon after school started and immediately, the four of us decided to pursue this idea—this dream of organizing our own 'Pay It Forward' tour and taking a bus of students from Minneapolis to Washington, D.C., over spring break," Brian explains. "We knew that any group of three people with $15 can form their own student organization on campus, and with a lot of passion, hard work, time, and dedication, together we founded and developed the student organization called Students Today Leaders Forever . . . to make our dream a reality."

Starting Your Own Campus Group

When starting a group on your own, a key ingredient is people power. If you have a friend who feels the same as you about the need for a new campus group, you'll have an easier time recruiting members and going through the start-up procedures. Most schools have a formal process through which students must apply, either through student government, or the office of student activities, for recognition as an official campus group. University recognition gives a group the right to post flyers on campus and be listed in directories, as well as receive office space, a Web page, and most importantly, some funding.

The foursome, all members of the class of 2007, cultivated a perfect storm of enthusiasm and commitment. They obtained their official campus charter within a month, and less than six months later, their "Pay It Forward" tour, with 33 Minnesota students, zipped toward the nation's capitol. "We worked with local kids in Chicago, helped with a huge inner-city cleanup project in Canton, worked at a food bank in Greensburg, Pennsylvania, talked with people on the streets of West Philadelphia about how they can get help finding housing and employment, and worked at a soup kitchen in D.C.," says Brian. They even met elected officials such as Pennsylvania Governor Edward G. Rendell on their journey.

Word has spread, and now students at other colleges around the country have expressed interest in starting their own "Pay It Forward" tours.

Should I join a fraternity or sorority?

If ever there was a college decision that rests on individual preferences, this is it. Despite its popularity on many campuses, the Greek system eludes a single description that all students agree on. Those who belong to fraternities and sororities almost universally espouse their social, academic, and personal benefits. Those who aren't members may be supportive—they have friends who are Greek, they sometimes go to parties, or their interactions have been positive. On the other hand, they may dislike the system's selective nature, costs, and occasional excesses.

As fraternities and sororities vary from college to college and within each campus, no single experience can be predicted for a school's Greek system. Current students say incoming freshmen are better off waiting until they get to campus and then finding out on their own if fraternity or sorority membership is right for them.

During the fall of his sophomore year, Jamie Simchik (Colgate University, Class of 2007) participated in "rush"—a period, at the start of semesters, of visiting different houses and sampling Greek life in hopes of finding a match. Jamie made a good impression, receiving bids from four fraternities, but he ended up turning them down.

"Socially, the Greek system is great for some people and limiting to others," says Jamie. "In my case, I felt it would have been lim ting. I am currently involved in a variety of different activities and groups on campus and my social circle is almost campus-wide. I wanted to hang out with who I wanted to hang out with when I wanted to hang out with them." He's aware that fraternity membership, while by no means prohibiting involvement in other campus activities, can in some cases cut into one's time to get involved elsewhere on campus.

Jamie says his overall impression of the system is positive, and he remains close with many friends who are in fraternities. He's been able to see firsthand that Greeks aren't cut off from outside contact. And he knows they have a great value on campus, not only because of their parties, but because of the good things they do, such as volunteerism. But in the end, he decided that he'd rather not join.

> *"I chose not to rush—but not because I dislike the system. I found a group of great friends my very first week of school and I still have those friends. When rush came along I didn't feel I had the need to make an entire house of new friends. Some people rush but not pledge; that is always a possibility and it helps you find out what the Greek system is like. I don't recommend writing off the Greek system before you even experience it or speak to people who have pledged. Those who are in it usually say it is the best thing ever."*
>
> —Alyssa Limberakis, Syracuse University, Class of 2006

John Andersen (University of Missouri–Columbia, Class of 2007) is one of those students who came this close to writing off the Greek system without inspecting it firsthand. He received information in the mail before freshman year even started. "Coming from a small town, all I had heard were stereotypes and I threw the recruiting material away before I even looked at it," he says. But one day in October he saw a flyer on a bulletin board announcing a new fraternity and giving him the chance to be a founding father. "All it pitched was an informational meeting, so I figured, 'why not?'"

He connected right away with others at the meeting. "I decided that this was right for me and I ended up joining and not regretting one minute of it."

Irene Fernando, one of four cofounders of the Students Today Leaders Forever group at the University of Minnesota, Twin Cities, faced the same situation. She was well aware of the "stigmas" associated with Greek life, and struggled with her decision to rush, but she decided she had to find out for herself what it's all about.

She found out that the stereotypes were wrong, and that being a sister did not limit her ability to do other things, especially her time-consuming efforts on behalf of Students Today Leaders Forever. "They have been a constant source of love and support," Irene says of her sorority sisters. "If I wanted to feed the homeless, have a movie night, or party like a rock star, they have always been there."

Nicholas Sauer (University of Denver, Class of 2005) says it's unfair to portray Greek life as a nonstop Bacchanalian feast. The image of Greeks being nothing but preppies and alcoholics is outdated, says Nicholas, who's also president of Theta Chi Fraternity and DU's Interfraternity Council. "Greeks around the nation are acting in communities, working with children, and promoting good study habits."

Pros and Cons of Joining a Fraternity or Sorority

Pros	*Cons*
You'll have a constant source of friends throughout your college years and beyond.	Some fraternities and sororities may present an air of exclusivity, with limited chances to interact with those who are different.
The chapter house will serve as a home where "brothers" or "sisters" will always be—something that can't be said of dorm life, where most faces and names change every year.	The costs can be daunting—a one-time initiation fee followed by regular dues. High insurance premiums that fraternities and sororities must pay are partly responsible for this. Living in the chapter house, however, does not usually cost significantly more than a college's standard room and board fees.
The social life affords frequent opportunities to mingle with the opposite sex.	While Greek life may not be as wild as some movies make it out to be, the allegations that they sometimes overemphasize partying and alcohol are not without merit.
You will get involved in charity endeavors—something you may aspire to do but never actually take the time to do on your own.	Some students will find the commitment overwhelming; although they're free to socialize with others, they may feel that they do not have the freedom to really stretch their wings.

continued

Pros and Cons of Joining a Fraternity or Sorority (continued)	
Pros	***Cons***
Greek life provides many chances to build leadership and personal-growth skills, through organizing events, coordinating communications, and working with a team. Also, academics are emphasized; many houses pride themselves on having cumulative grade-point averages above the campus-wide average.	The hazing issue has haunted the Greek system—mostly fraternities—for years. In one of the more recent cases, Walter Dean Jennings, a freshman fraternity pledge at Plattsburgh State University in New York, died of water intoxication in 2003 after a hazing stunt in which he was forced to consume large quantities of water through a funnel. Eleven fraternity brothers eventually pleaded guilty to various charges, and the house was banned from campus. While the hazing problem has largely abated, its ugly face surfaces on occasion.

Holly Woodhead (Gettysburg College, Class of 2005) has experienced life inside and outside of the Greek system. She wrestled with her decision to rush during the fall of her sophomore year, at a time when many of her upperclassmen friends were already part of sororities. She weighed the possible social benefits against the costs and decided to pledge a sorority when she received a bid.

"Not long after pledging started did I realize that I had made a mistake," she recalls. For starters, none of her friends were also in the same sorority, so she was on her own. She did not feel a smooth connection with some of her sorority sisters. Lastly, she felt she wasn't able to give her schoolwork the attention it deserved. "I decided that I no longer wanted to belong to the sorority."

She was deeply concerned about her exit plan, but she moved ahead and did what she thought was best. "After planning what I was going to say to the pledgemaster and president, I spoke to them about the situation" she remembers. "I will never forget how nervous I was going to the senior's house off campus. To my surprise they were very understanding and respected my decision. To this day, I still have friends who are in the sorority and no one has given me a hard time about the situation."

When she looks back, Holly realizes that she overestimated how "uncool" it would be to not join a sorority. "From a firsthand experience I can tell you that that is not the case," she says. "Your social life is what you make of it. The key is having high self-esteem, a strong character, and a positive self-image."

So, should you rush a fraternity or sorority? It comes down to your personal choice. Meredith Schweitzer (Vanderbilt University, Class of 2006) insists there's a Greek house that fits everyone's personality—but they must take the initiative to check the houses out.

"For someone who is going away to college . . . your sorority or fraternity can be a home away from home. I think being in a sorority is one of the best decisions I have made in my college career. Greek life can open up the door for numerous opportunities. It is something you can take with you after college and still be involved in as a working professional."

—Sara Adcock, University of Memphis, Class of 2005

How can I continue my religion's observances?

For many students, going away to college disrupts a routine that's been part of their lives as long as they can remember: attendance at weekly religious services with their families. Whether they daydreamed through services or took active roles, it was always understood that at one set time each weekend—maybe Saturday afternoons at 5, or Sunday mornings at 10—the family would unite for worship. In college, such observances are optional; Dad isn't threatening to withhold the car keys if you don't get out of bed to attend services.

The situation illustrates how the freedoms of college life are often accompanied by complex choices. Whether they realize it or not, all students make a decision about religion when they go away to college. Some drift away, or continue to stay away, from religion—maybe they get caught up in socializing or academics, or maybe they reject some fundamental ideas. Others embrace a religion or reaffirm the commitment made in ceremonies such as confirmation or bar/bat mitzvah—they elect to become adult participants in their religious community.

> *"Perhaps the best and worst place in the world to have faith is on a college campus. Like it or not, there are lots of parties, drinking, sex, and activities that might not fit with your moral code. And it's very easy to get sucked into that world. On the other hand, if you choose to be faithful, there are huge Christian and non-Christian student unions everywhere. You can find any faith you want, and the best part is that nobody really cares about how you classify yourself."*
>
> —Erin Malony, University of Kentucky, Class of 2007

Those interested in continuing their observances will find they are able to do so. It's mostly like home but with at least a few differences: At on-campus chapels, almost all of the congregants are fellow students instead of the usual intergenerational mix. Additionally, as a result, religious leaders who are mindful of their audience tend to target their sermons directly to the students, making them easier to relate to.

Sticking to a family tradition, Tanner Sykes (Texas Tech University, Class of 2005) attends the First Presbyterian Church in Lubbock; his parents and grandparents attended the church when they went to Tech, and his great-grandfather was a minister there. He says that "connection" to the church makes him feel welcome, and keeps him coming back.

Tanner admits, however, that it's not always easy to attend church as a college student on the go. "I've always been a strong Presbyterian member of my hometown church, but after coming to college, attending church on Sunday morning is much more difficult than before," Tanner says. "A late night of partying will make it much more difficult to wake up early Sunday morning. However, it is possible to continue to observe your religion's routines if you plan to attend and don't deviate."

Matthew Weber (Class of 2006) chose to attend Providence College in part because it is a Roman Catholic–affiliated institution. He regularly attends mass there, but points out that students decide how much to make religion a part of their lives. Matthew says that upon his arrival at Providence, "I soon realized that the Catholic aspect to any school can be completely embraced or totally ignored."

He has many friends on campus from different religious backgrounds, including those who are Jewish, Episcopalian, and atheist. "In any case, everyone of every faith embraces differences and most of all, respects each other."

Ryan Renz (Indiana University of Pennsylvania, Class of 2005) has found a similarly hospitable religious environment. The college has several centers where students attend services, he explains. "There is also an organization for just about every religion on our campus."

At the University of Kentucky, students may be challenged about their beliefs, but they're also free to express those beliefs, says Erin Malony. "It all comes down to choice—if you want to be devout, you can be. And there's lots of support and encouragement for that," she says. "And if you don't, there's a place for that, too."

10

Alcohol

> *All of this sounds like complete and utter common sense, but it is incredible how many people don't listen to common-sense ideas.*
>
> —John Andersen, University of Missouri–Columbia, Class of 2007

Samantha Spady, a member of Colorado State University's Class of 2006, could easily be compared to many students cited in this book. Samantha was an honor student in her Nebraska high school, and had been class president, cheerleading captain, and homecoming queen. At Colorado State, she was a business major and gifted sketch artist with a promising future.

Nineteen-year-old Samantha Spady was found dead in a fraternity house at 6:22 p.m. on September 5, 2004. Her body apparently lay in a lounge unnoticed for at least 12 hours. With a blood-alcohol level of .436, she had enough alcohol in her system to make five people drunk, according to information provided by investigators. The police and coroner concluded that she had consumed at least 30 drinks, including final gulps from a bottle of vanilla-flavored vodka. The official cause of her death: acute ethanol poisoning.

In the aftermath, the predictable actions followed: The university disbanded the fraternity. Students and administrators somberly spoke of deep sadness and vowed to make changes. A candlelight vigil took place on campus. Alcohol was banned at all Greek houses, and sales were suspended at home football games.

But no eulogies or promises or candles or rallies or tears would bring Samantha back. To see her alive, one could check out her Yahoo.com picture page. There, under her screen name, sambamboogie, one sees a college student who looks so much like any other that it's frightening. The photos show her with friends in dozens of scenes—hanging out at parties, having fun, and smiling—always smiling. Samantha was a young woman full of life.

She should not be dead.

Samantha's case is not isolated. The *Denver Post* reported at least nine other instances in the previous year in which college students died as a direct result of excessive alcohol abuse. That does not count the thousands who needed medical intervention as a result of excessive drinking.

There are myriad lessons to draw from Samantha's death. Let's start with two:

- ✓ Alcohol can be deadly, especially to those who underestimate its destructive abilities.
- ✓ Tragedies involving alcohol very frequently happen to good, friendly, vivacious, caring students—the kind you'd be proud to call a brother or sister, and the kind who are exactly like you.

This chapter examines one of the most critical social decisions college students face: whether to drink, and if so, how to handle it.

How can I have fun if everyone around me is drinking?

Expect alcohol to be a big part of college life, whether or not you personally drink. Despite age restrictions, students will sneak alcohol into their dorms, including, especially, freshman dorms. Students find a way to drink at bars, whether they use fake IDs to get in, or whether they simply have an upperclassman buy drinks for them. And easiest of all, the beer and booze flow freely at off-campus parties.

If it's Thursday, Friday, or Saturday night—or any of the other nights, depending on the school and its culture—you won't have to look hard to find students drinking. But many realize there are

Drinking and Friends

You don't drink, but your friends do. You may not need to give up your friends, but you should make sure your friendship isn't lopsided. Consider the answers to these questions. No magical grading scale exists to tell you whether you need new friends—honest answers will make it very clear.

- ✓ Do they pressure you to drink?
- ✓ Does their entire social life revolve around drinking, or is drinking only one aspect of it?
- ✓ Are these people, or at least some of them, occasionally willing to do things your way—perhaps a movie night that doesn't involve drinking?
- ✓ Do they take for granted your willingness to be the designated driver, or to help them out when trouble arises? Do you frequently feel like you're the only responsible member of the group?

numerous other ways to socialize—or that they can hang out with friends who are drinking without feeling the need to partake themselves. In short, no matter how prevalent drinking is on campus, those who don't wish to drink always have other choices.

It wasn't long before Cody Quintero (University of Kansas, Class of 2007) found himself alone on his dorm's floor because just about everyone else was into drinking. Cody wanted no part of it. He was paying his way through KU, and did not want to jeopardize his education by drinking himself into trouble.

He quickly faced the fact that he wouldn't be best friends with his floormates. No big deal. At the same time, though, he began getting involved, joining KU's chapter of the Association of University Residence Halls. Such groups exist on most residential campuses, and offer a great outlet to partake in leadership and programming activities. [Cody explained some of the benefits of his AURH involvement in the previous chapter.]

"That is where you will meet your friends," says Cody. "The best thing was when I got involved I met people who were passionate about what they were doing, and none of them drank. So I was allowed to surround myself with friends and a life that didn't include drinking." Cody and his friends regularly take advantage of the many programs on campus, such as speakers, or they'll spend a night on the town, going out to the movies. And sometimes they just enjoy hanging out. The funny part is that it's not so different from what people do when they're drinking—it's just that there's no alcohol involved.

When it comes to hanging out or going to parties, students should be able to enjoy themselves and the company of others regardless of their beverage choice. Those who stick with Diet Coke for the night often don't care if their friends are drinking beer, as long as those "friends" don't make them feel awkward for their choice.

No one is going to pressure Bowling Green State University student Aaron Turner to drink, for example. He won't stand for it. "I . . . would rather stay home and chat on the Internet than feel uncomfortable at a party," says Aaron (Class of 2005).

Good friends will be glad to have you around no matter what, says Lauren Hardgrove (Ohio University, Class of 2005). "If the people who you are with are truly your friends, then they will understand that you do not want to drink."

Despite the common perception, not all college students drink, points out Adam Ritton (Creighton University, Class of 2007).

Who Cares What's In Your Cup?

A creeping sense of awkwardness might persist if you're the only one at a party without a drink in your hand. Even well-intentioned friends who badger, "Wanna drink?" can annoy after a while. Megan Thompson (University of Idaho, Class of 2006) has a solution: Put a drink in your hand—a non-alcoholic one. "I've found that drinking something such as soda, water, or juice helps . . . because then you also have something to keep your hands occupied," says Megan.

"If you want to have fun but don't want to drink, there are literally thousands of other students who feel the same way as you do," says Adam. He found a roughly even split freshman year on his dorm's floor. "Every student had a choice on which side they wanted to party at for that evening, and either way, both sides had a great time."

Bethany Sheldon (Boston University, Class of 2006) has no difficulty passing on alcohol when she goes out to a party or club with her friends. She sees lots of practical benefits to not drinking. "It's really not fun to be drunk all the time because often when you wake up the next day, you won't remember half the stuff you did when you were drunk, and you get hangovers," she says. "And, you can definitely have fun without drinking."

Some people say that it's easier to loosen up when you're drinking. While there's some truth to that, Bethany says it's pretty easy to relax and be yourself if you're not drinking and others are. They're likely saying or doing silly things, putting you in the mood to laugh and have a good time.

Lots of students echo Bethany's thoughts on this aspect of staying sober—they say that their friends provide more than enough material to keep the nights interesting.

Kristen Watts (University of Texas at Austin, Class of 2006) suggests getting those friends out on the dance floor, for example. "As a student-athlete who has chosen to abstain from alcohol, and to put my health, academics, athletics, and yes, even social life, ahead of 'getting totally wasted,' I've found that it's easy to say no to alcohol and still have an awesome time wherever I am," says Kristen, who belongs to the rowing team. "Believe me, you can have a ton of fun without the alcohol, and—guess what?—you'll remember it the next day."

As a Mormon, Catherine Anne Bennion doesn't drink, but she agrees that dancing is something that drinkers and nondrinkers can do together—although the sober ones have better coordination. Catherine, who transferred from Vanderbilt University to Brigham Young University in the spring of 2005, doesn't mind going to parties where alcohol is served, but avoids those where it's the focal point. She suggests going to parties where other things are going on, such as dancing or playing pool.

"My best advice is to go to parties, where you know there'll be a lot of alcohol, with a good friend who knows and appreciates your limits and your decision," she says. "Pretty soon everyone else will know where you stand, and the drink offers will dissipate. . . . People won't respect you any less if you just tell them you're not interested."

While the sober souls in the crowd may not embrace the role of babysitter, they often take comfort in the fact that at least someone is in control if something goes wrong. "Although this may not sound like fun, if you are sober, you can stop someone who has been drinking from doing something stupid, like driving, or take care of someone who is sick," says Bethany Sheldon of Boston University. "You might end up saving someone's life."

Benefits to Steering Clear of Alcohol

- ✓ Your judgment won't be affected. Intoxication, by its very nature, removes one's sense of good judgment and coordination, making you more susceptible to misfortune or tragedy. Staying sober eliminates that risk.
- ✓ You'll avoid the agony of hangovers.
- ✓ You won't end up sick to your stomach and vomiting on your dorm's bathroom floor. And you won't have to clean up that mess in the morning, either. [Word usually gets out about who was resposible for such messes, and floormates will insist you clean it.]
- ✓ There's no chance you'll drive drunk—meaning you won't be arrested for it, and you won't maim or kill somebody as a result of drunk driving.
- ✓ Drinking is expensive. Bypass it and you'll save plenty of cash.
- ✓ You'll prove to yourself and others that the "real" you is the one worth knowing, and that you don't need to be drunk to be amusing.

Says Adam Abelkop (Wake Forest University, Class of 2007): "It's nice to be appreciated for being the DD [designated driver]—you're the most important person at the party."

Consider, however, the limits of looking out for defiant, reckless friends. Urge them not to do something stupid, and threaten to alert authorities if you must, but you should not have to put your personal safety at risk if they refuse to heed your warnings.

James Smith (University of Maryland, Class of 2006) brings a unique perspective to student use of alcohol. He's older than most students—he attended a community college and served four years in the Marine Corps before enrolling at College Park. He knows excessive drinking will only hinder his efforts to succeed, so he doesn't do it. "I don't think it helps me out any," says James, who is studying architecture and art history. "When I came into college, I had already gotten out of that phase. I want to learn—drugs and alcohol are going to restrict that."

How should I handle alcohol?

As most college students can tell you, there's a big difference between drinking and getting drunk. "I have a saying that I learned my freshman year at DU: 'Drinking in moderation beats vomiting in excess,'" says Nicholas Sauer (University of Denver, Class of 2005). "Knowing the limit and being able to handle oneself responsibly is what college is about—it's a learning process."

Keep in mind that if you're driving, there is no safe amount of alcohol to imbibe, despite the fact that legal sanctions may not kick in until you have passed a certain blood-alcohol threshold. (Some states have zero-tolerance policies for young drivers.) But forget about the law for a moment: You could kill someone or be killed if you drink and drive. That is all the incentive you need to never get behind the wheel after drinking.

Even if you happen to be legally sober, if you have the misfortune of being in a car accident—one that wasn't your fault—you absolutely do not want the police to smell those two cups of beer or fruity spiked punch on your breath at the accident scene. Your credibility will be zero and police at the scene will be skeptical of your account—who could blame them? As a college student who smells like alcohol, you'll be put on the defense, no matter what the circumstances.

Everyone has different limits when it comes to drinking, but a general rule of thumb is to have no more than one drink an hour; those with smaller builds, such as a woman who weighs 115 pounds, have an even lower limit.

A "drink" is generally defined as a 12-ounce can of beer, a 5-ounce glass of wine, or 1.5 ounces of 80-proof liquor.

Other variables include exactly what kind of beer, wine, or spirits you're drinking, as well as the serving size. If you're drinking beer out of one of those ubiquitous red plastic 16-ounce cups, it counts as one-and-a-third beers—you should have at most two over a three-hour period. And if you're drinking a strong punch-type concoction out of a giant cup, you could easily be consuming two or more "drinks" at once.

To avoid anything like that situation, John Andersen and his buddies at the University of Missouri–Columbia always take precautions. "Between my friends and me, we always have a person who is our designated driver—not because we know that we are going to become completely drunk, but because we know that zero tolerance means zero tolerance, and a DUI can practically ruin your life," he says. "No matter if you plan on getting drunk or not, if you know you are going to have a drink, you should turn your keys over. All of this sounds like complete and utter common sense, but it is incredible how many people don't listen to common-sense ideas."

It may seem obvious, but students strongly advise staying with good friends when you drink. That's easier to do when you start drinking than it is later on, when parties get more crowded and you may have consumed more than you can handle.

If you get separated, find your friends right away or go home.

Bryant Jones (University of Vermont, Class of 2005) has seen some pathetic sights involving drunken students at his school: "I have been to parties and seen people throwing up over toilets and vomiting on themselves, and nobody was there with them," he says. "My best advice if you want to go out to a party is to go with friends you can trust and don't leave friends behind or let a friend go off with a stranger, no matter how nice that stranger has been to your friend over the last few beers."

Bryant points out the coexisting allure and danger of drinking at college: While your parents aren't keeping tabs on you, or expecting you home at a certain time, there's also no one keeping your behavior in check the way they might have done, he explains. For example, in high school, if you were up to no good with your friends at midnight, you might have gotten into deeper trouble by staying out later, but you went home because you knew that arriving past 12:30 would mean you'd forfeit your car privileges.

In college, no such fail-safe exists. "Always rely on yourself to not get drunk if you don't want to," recommends Debra Trevino (University of Texas at Austin, Class of 2005).

Your friends may help you avoid trouble sometimes, but don't expect them to keep a constant watch over you. Despite their promises, they may not always be there.

When it comes to drinking, keep some ground rules in mind:

- ✓ **Ask yourself why you're drinking.** Dr. Sharon Levy of Harvard Medical School, who is cited extensively in the next chapter on other drugs, says the answer will reveal whether you should reconsider drinking or seek professional help. If you're exhausted at the end of a long week of academics and plan to go out drinking as a "reward," for example, you're probably much better off taking it easy and resting. Those who use alcohol or other drugs as stress relief, or to help themselves relax or change their moods, are headed down the wrong path. "These are warning signs," Dr. Levy says.
- ✓ **Trying to "catch up" to other drinkers is a sure way to take on more alcohol than you can handle.** Drink at a pace that keeps you sober, regardless of how others are drinking.
- ✓ **The only way to avoid a hangover is by not getting drunk.** Keep that in mind if you think you have a class the next morning. "Professors know the difference between a hung-over student and one who is just tired," says Jessica Martin of Western Kentucky University.
- ✓ **Avoid alcoholic punches and similar concoctions for which you know nothing about either the ingredients or their proportions**. Some may be so heavily spiked that a single cup can make you sick or knock you on your backside.

✓ **Similarly, never leave your drink unattended—especially if you're in the midst of hooking up with someone you don't know well.** Take it with you to the bathroom if you must. So-called date-rape drugs such as Rohypnol and GHB are not just something you hear about on *Dateline NBC*. These drugs are a persistent threat, especially to college women. They can render victims incapacitated within a short period of time and unable to consent to sex. Alcohol is also a leading factor in rape, covered in more detail in Chapter 12.

✓ **Alcohol lowers inhibitions, to use a technical phrase.** In practical terms, this means a drunk is much more likely to dance on a table, start a brawl over a perceived slight, or end up sleeping with a stranger. It could result in embarrassment, a broken jaw, or a sexually transmitted disease. And yes, it may result in nothing at all—but that's the very nature of risk.

✓ **If you drink alone, drink just to get drunk, have trouble limiting your drinking, or if your drinking is affecting your schoolwork, seek professional help.** This takes on greater urgency if depression or physical risk is ever part of the equation. Seeking help doesn't mean you're a basket case, by any means—it's a sign that you want to take charge of your life before alcohol does. Colleges take a leading role in society in making nonjudgmental assistance available to those who want to turn things around. Start with your resident adviser, who can point you in the right direction. Everything can be done in confidence. But students must take the first step. Those who wait for the university's recommendation may have waited too long.

✓ **If you sense you're on the verge of doing something that might cause irreparable harm—whether it's driving, damaging property, performing a dangerous stunt, or even committing suicide—confess to someone you can trust that you immediately need someone to care for you or watch you constantly.** Call the campus police for assistance, if you must. If it's your first time placing such a call, any possible consequences would likely be minimal, especially compared to the possible consequences of not calling.

✓ **Likewise, if you're at a gathering—whether you're drunk or sober—and any kind of bad situation develops, grab your friends and leave.** If you have a bad feeling in your gut, trust it and get out.

Drinking is filled with contradictions: It can make a sad person appear happy, while his grief actually intensifies beneath the surface. It can make a shy person violent. And it can make a straight-A student risk his life to accomplish a silly stunt. Yet at the same time, many students who get drunk regularly still get strong grades and are otherwise well-rounded.

It's tough to make sense out of it all. But alcohol is a numbers game, and the numbers are wholly unpredictable—just like a drunken student. Students should watch their drinking not because they'll definitely die or definitely fail out if they don't. They should watch their drinking because it's an indisputable fact that those bad things *are much more likely to happen* when their senses (or those of the people they hang out with) are impaired. Again, it's a matter of risk, and the stakes are nothing less than your life.

> *"Many students become alcoholics in college and don't even realize it until they graduate. Others sacrifice their grades for bar life. I'm not saying not to drink, I am just saying that you should always be aware when you are drinking too often or too much."*
>
> —Catherine Bell, University of Kansas, Class of 2004

Every year, the nation's leading universities kick students out because of their drinking. Alcohol may not be the stated reason, of course, but the underlying causes are connected to it: pulling a fire alarm, damaging property, assaulting another student, violating dormitory rules, or receiving poor grades, for example.

> Whether you're drinking or not, to avoid becoming an innocent victim of a fight or accident, know your surroundings—from the people you're hanging out with and the neighborhood you're visiting, to the overall safety of the situation and the nearest exit. If something's not right, put your safety first—either don't go in the first place or leave as soon as you can.

Lastly, if the prospect of physical harm or getting thrown out of school isn't a disincentive to avoid alcohol abuse, the immediate prospect of a hangover might do the trick. For many students, the "fun" of drinking pales in contrast to what follows: the acidic agony of throwing up at 3 a.m.; waking up with an unquenchable thirst as well as "cotton mouth" at 7 a.m.; sleeping half the following day away; and coping with a brain-rattling headache most of the next day.

It's enough to make one wonder why anyone gets drunk more than once.

Erica Lemansky of Brandeis University's Class of 2005 knows it's a valuable attribute to know when to stop drinking: "You may think you are cool when you are throwing back your fifth beer, but when your new roommate is holding your hair back in the bathroom, your sudden 'coolness' will disappear," she says. "The life of the party is not the one who has taken the most shots—so be smart, but of course, have a good time."

Should I get a fake ID?

The blistering pace of the first weeks of college life can drain any memory of the wise words imparted during freshman orientation, back in August. But some things, inexplicably, stick. Bethany Sheldon remembers a presentation given by the campus police at Boston University's orientation for new students. She never forgot it.

"They pulled out a shopping bag full of probably over 500 fake IDs that they had confiscated and dumped them all over the stage of the auditorium," and then they followed up with an explanation of what happens to those who get caught with them, she recalls. "I decided right then that it wasn't worth it at all to spend money on an ID that would probably get me into trouble."

Many ignored the advice, including a good friend of hers. She spent $80 for two fake ID cards that Bethany thought looked just as credible as a real driver's license.

It turns out they weren't credible enough.

When her friend presented the ID at a liquor store near campus, the clerk, not willing to risk the store's liquor license, confiscated it. He knew it was fake. Bethany's friend ended up spending the next few weeks worrying that she might be arrested.

While it didn't come to that, it very easily could have.

"To me, having [a fake] ID isn't worth the risk of getting caught," says Alyssa Limberakis (Syracuse University, Class of 2006). "I never got an ID and I don't feel like I missed out on anything super or amazing." Echoing the situation at many college campuses, she points out that the Syracuse city police have made a concerted effort to curb underage student drinking by raiding bars and asking all patrons to produce ID. A series of raids conducted as part of "Operation Prevent" in 2003 resulted in dozens of citations.

To understand the severity of possessing fake ID, it might help to explain the offense's more bureaucratic name: possession of a forged government document. That's what might appear on your arrest record.

The crime may be a felony, depending on the circumstances of the arrest and the means employed to obtain the ID. While you probably won't be sent up the river for a first offense, a conviction may put you on thin ice. In other words, a second conviction on a related charge—indicating you did not learn your lesson the first time—could very possibly lead to jail time. Laws differ considerably from state to state, and in some areas, the penalties are still minimal. But the trend points toward increased penalties, especially in college towns where drinking is a problem. Terrorism concerns have also lead authorities to adopt a zero-tolerance position toward those who forge government documents for any reason.

"If you get caught, you have to go to court, and it is a whole big mess," Alyssa says. And those court dates? Some were scheduled right in the middle of spring break.

If police raid a bar or house party, underage drinkers can be arrested or given a summons for merely possessing alcoholic beverages—even if they did not use false ID to get them. Those who abstain from drinking may also get swept up in raids—the cops might not believe their cups contain only soda.

What if I get busted for alcohol in my dorm?

Despite all the freedoms college students have, and their right to do as they please in their dorm rooms, there are limits. Specifically, you can't host a beer bash in your room. And if you're under the legal age, you're not allowed to drink.

It may seem hard to believe, but there was a time, before most states raised the drinking age to 21 in the 1980s, when students could cheerfully get a beer with their dinner in the dining halls. And alcohol use in the dorms was virtually unmonitored. Those days, however, are long gone.

For reasons of student safety and legal obligations, schools have cracked down on underage drinking in dorms. Enforcement varies among different colleges, but if lots of people are shuffling in and out of a dorm room, the sounds of Jim Morrison and The Doors are blasting, and loud chants of "GO! GO! GO!" are rattling through the hallways, one can expect a firm knock on the door from the Resident Adviser.

When the door opens (it'll be too late to lower the music and pretend no one's home), her first words probably won't be, "Can I join in the fun?"

What usually follows is a not-so-subtle reminder that although you don't have to answer to your parents anymore, you do have to answer to your school's designated authority.

The good news is that getting written up by your R.A. is not as bad as getting busted by the cops. It won't result in a summons or a criminal record, of course. But colleges are mindful of the dangers of drinking—from rape to destruction of campus property to suicide. They want to prevent those things from happening. In the same capacity, they want to prove to parents that their college isn't a place where heavy drinking and its accompanying tragedies are tolerated.

Many schools take a "rehabilitative" approach to alcohol violations, with the goal of teaching students the dangers of alcohol abuse. Such students may be asked to write a report about their drinking, attend a seminar for policy violators, or possibly, pay a fine. At Western Kentucky University, Jessica Martin reports that students must write a letter home to their parents explaining the situation and attend an Alcoholics Anonymous meeting.

Repeat violators may be dealt with more harshly. They may be kicked out of campus housing, or kicked out of school. And, of course, alcohol-related stunts like fooling with elevators or setting off a fire alarm typically result in immediate expulsion—your school won't give any student another opportunity to engage in such life-threatening high jinks.

As a student security aide at the University of Kansas, Cody Quintero has encountered plenty of students who were drinking when they weren't supposed to. The confrontations have the potential to get ugly, but those who are drinking should know they won't prevail, and fess up.

"The best thing to remember is to be cooperative," he suggests. "If you fight back or have an attitude with the R.A. or staff member who catches you, it will only make matters worse for you in the end."

Incident reports are always drawn up based on these events, and the R.A.s note all the surrounding details, including the students' attitudes. "If a complex director reads a report where the student was cooperative and didn't put up a fight, he or she is more likely to let the student off more easily than someone who was resisting the incident."

11

Other Drugs

> *If you try something that has been laced, then you may end up sick or even dead. It is not a risk worth taking.*
>
> —Lauren Hardgrove, Ohio University, Class of 2005

Students learn about themselves in college by doing new things and pushing boundaries. Perhaps that's why many who would never dream of breaking the law or endangering their lives might otherwise try drugs. Some convince themselves nothing bad can come of it. They are emboldened by the fact that, despite all the warnings about drugs, they know people on campus who have tried or even regularly use drugs—and they haven't dropped dead yet. What these students may not stop to think about, though, are the many wasted lives that resulted from similar rationalizations.

This chapter will take a look at drugs other than alcohol on campus, and how students have handled choices associated with drug use. It relates how and why colleges have little tolerance for drug-using students, and it makes it clear, from a legal standpoint, the deep trouble that can result from a drug arrest. In addition, a Harvard Medical School faculty member with extensive research experience in the field tells why even trying drugs is a bad idea. Even once.

As a result, this chapter is less about making choices than the urgency of making the only practical choice about drugs: staying away from them at all cost.

Should I try pot or other drugs?

If you're not familiar with the smell of marijuana, you'll likely know it when you sniff its unmistakable pungent odor. Expect its scent to creep through the hallways if students are using it anywhere on your dorm floor. And if they open the door while you're passing by, you might receive a friendly invitation to join in.

Students say declining the offer is one of the best decisions you can make in college.

Grace Choe (University of Southern California, Class of 2005) says she realizes that trying drugs isn't likely to kill you. "But personally, I don't think drugs are that much of a hurrah—it's not worth it for me to [mess] up my mind. I have a pretty shoddy memory to begin with, so I like to keep all my brain cells, thank you."

Students say pot is the most commonly used drug on campus and, as a result, the one most likely to be offered to them. They might be enticed by claims that it's pure or "good stuff." They're mindful that pot isn't in the same league as drugs such as cocaine or Ecstasy, and the claims of quality reassure them.

One student not otherwise cited in this chapter suggests, "Make sure you know where it came from," to those thinking of trying pot. It seems like good advice, especially considering the source: an intelligent student who is cited in several other chapters in this book. But the guidance is flawed: First, you can't predict how you'll respond to getting high. Secondly, unless you personally grew it and manufactured it yourself (not impossible but unlikely), there is no way to know for certain where it "came from" or what's in it.

The only thing you can be sure of is that you're risking your health by inhaling such a substance.

Who does know what's in it? The criminal who's earning money by selling drugs. It shouldn't need to be pointed out that students usually wouldn't trust their well being to such people.

"You never know if these drugs are pure," says Lauren Hardgrove (Ohio University, Class of 2005), referring not just to pot but to all drugs. "Most of my friends have tried drugs and some have had very bad effects from them. What they thought was going to be a good time turned into a day-or-more nightmare. Just from hearing these stories, I know that it is not smart."

A marijuana joint, for example, could be laced with crack cocaine, heroin, or PCP, just to name a few possibilities. Ecstasy could be tainted with mescaline, methamphetamine, or codeine, according to authorities.

The possibilities are endless, both for the contents of drugs and the consequences of taking them. A person who tries a tainted drug might not learn what's in it until something goes wrong.

Bad reactions to drugs have caused some of Kim Miller's friends to either violently throw up or become so sedated that they needed to have their breathing checked. Kim (College of William and Mary, Class of 2005) says some have even had seizures.

> *"You are going to college to get an education and get a good job so you can make money. We all are. Taking drugs will stand in your way of achieving this goal; bottom line—do not do it. Anyone I've seen mess with heavy drugs ends up with a ruined life—if not permanently, at least for a while."*
>
> —Lindsay Haymes, Southwest Missouri State University, Class of 2006

An Ecstasy-induced seizure, for example, can ravage the body; if prolonged, it can deprive the brain of oxygen and cause permanent brain damage or death, according to Dr. Sharon Levy, a researcher and clinician at the Center for Adolescent Substance Abuse Research at Children's Hospital Boston, the primary pediatric teaching hospital of Harvard Medical School.

Dr. Levy, who holds clinical appointments in medicine and psychiatry at Children's Hospital and is an instructor in pediatrics at Harvard Medical School, cites two examples showing how pot—typically considered among the most benign illegal drugs—can harm a college student

✓ Unlike other drugs, marijuana is stored in the body's fat tissue, where it is released at a slow rate. As a result, regular users can test positive for use of the drug weeks after taking it. While it stays in the body, it's also believed to affect the brain's neurons. Some researchers link marijuana use to "amotivational syndrome"—basically the idea of being a slacker, unmotivated, and underachieving. Dr. Levy says it's no accident that frequent marijuana users "tend to not care about a lot of stuff."

✓ A growing amount of research supports the theory that marijuana use can be a "trigger" for schizophrenia, a mental disorder in which thought processes and emotions are disconnected. Dr. Levy explains this by pointing out that everyone has "triggers" for various diseases. In most cases, they remain latent. But just as harmful chemicals are known to boost one's latent risk of developing cancer, the marijuana-schizophrenia link is being increasingly substantiated by sound scientific research. "It's pretty clear these days that for some people, they may not have ever had this disorder in their lifetime" but for the drug use, Dr. Levy says.

If the possible effects of marijuana are not daunting, other drugs have the potential to devastate in grisly ways. Two examples:

✓ Cocaine can kill instantly. "You can use cocaine for the very first time and die of a heart attack right then and there, because it can constrict the blood vessels that lead to the heart [and] supply blood to the heart," Dr. Levy says. "It can happen to a person with a perfectly normal heart."

✓ Opiates, such as heroin, codeine (available in over-the-counter medicines), and the prescription drugs OxyContin and Vicodin, have such powerful addictive properties that it's impossible to be a casual, recreational user. "Almost anyone who starts experimenting" will feel the pull, Dr. Levy says.

There are not enough pages in this book to describe the many drugs that are abused on college campuses. What's known, though, is that drugs can be lethal. They can lead to dangerous and criminal behavior. And they can be addictive, draining users not only of their money, but of their personalities and lust for life. When students place increasing value on obtaining drugs and getting high, everything else that's important in life—family, friends, school—gets left behind.

Alan S. Kastler (Southwest Missouri State University, Class of 2005) never considered taking that first step. He says he's heard the suggestions that "you should try marijuana and other drugs so that you know that doing drugs is not the right thing to do," but rejects them. Alan says he doesn't need to try drugs to learn anything: "That is how some people start using drugs and then do not stop."

Paul Campbell (University of New Mexico, Class of 2005) is another who isn't taking any chances. "The consequences for the use of drugs are too great for me," says Paul. "Personally, I dislike what effects drugs have on people. I have witnessed too many people turn down the dark road of drug abuse and addiction."

He's bothered when others smoke pot or use other drugs because he has to deal with the effects. He can't stand the smell of marijuana, for example, but when people smoke it in his dorm, the ventilation system circulates the smoke through the entire building. "So everyone's room smells of dope," he adds disdainfully.

Like the substances mentioned in this chapter, alcohol is also a drug. In many ways the same suggestions apply to both alcohol and other drugs. But there are some additional reasons to avoid drugs other than alcohol at all cost.

- ✓ Drugs such as cocaine are patently illegal under any circumstances. The penalty for possession of more than an ounce of some drugs can be a felony with years of mandatory prison time.
- ✓ Since drugs are illegal, their manufacturers operate outside the law. In short, you have no idea what's in the stuff you're using, and you're dealing with shady people when you buy drugs.
- ✓ Even alcohol, *when consumed in moderation,* is not harmful to those who do not have a pre-existing condition that rules out its use. No such claims can be made about illicit drugs—a single sample can kill.

Drugs and Your Development

Dr. Sharon Levy, who has treated hundreds of young people with drug problems, and conducted extensive research in the field, points out two realities that college students should confront when they're thinking about drugs:

- ✓ They are still developing on different levels—their bodies are still changing, their minds are still developing, and their interpersonal skills are still taking shape.
- ✓ Drug use interferes with that process.

The result of drug use among college students is often what you might expect when critical growth is disturbed—people get "hung up in their adolescence," unable to function as mature, independent adults as they move into their 20s and beyond, Dr. Levy explains. This information is not a vague theory—it's the result of research into the factors that have caused some people to flounder through adulthood. The link to drug use is incontrovertible.

In contrast, to make her point more clear, Dr. Levy states that a 36-year-old healthy male, for example, would be at a much lower risk if he tried marijuana than a 19-year-old college student, precisely because the 36-year-old is fully mature. "The most risky time to use drugs is during adolescence," including the college years, says Dr. Levy, who is also an instructor in pediatrics at Harvard Medical School. She recognizes that college students might bristle at any suggestion that they are adolescents, but encourages them to see why younger college students, especially, fall into this category: "I see college students as . . . still in transition. They're starting to take responsibility, but still need a lot of support. . . . They're clearly not in the same place as when they were 16, but in a transitional zone. I see [adolescence] as being over when you're a fully independent person."

What consequences can I expect if I take drugs?

Unless you obtained your alcohol with a forged government document, the penalties for being caught drinking while underage, while unpleasant, are relatively mild. It's not something to aspire to, of course, but the worst you're usually looking at is a summons.

It's different with drugs, despite whether a student is caught by city police or campus representatives.

Illinois State University, for example, has an alcohol policy consistent with that found at many schools: first-time offenders receive a warning, while second-time offenders must attend a four-hour educational program as well as an initial substance-abuse screening. Only on the third and subsequent violations are students subject to university probation, suspension, or expulsion. But when it comes to drugs, even sometimes-lightly regarded marijuana, the penalties are harsher: a year's probation, a fine, mandatory attendance at an education program, and notification of parents in most cases for students under 21—just for the first infraction. They must also prepare a reflection paper. Second-time violators may be suspended or expelled. Those caught distributing drugs face a one-semester suspension, and those caught selling drugs face a one-year suspension or outright dismissal.

Rick Olshak, the Illinois State associate dean of students, says the strict policies are in place to safeguard the No. 1 reason why students come to college in the first place: to get an education.

When a bright young student who shows up at Illinois State ends up dropping out, his grade report littered with C's, D's, and F's, Olshak all too often sees drugs, including alcohol, as the leading factor. "Is it because this person suddenly became stupid?" he asks students when giving presentations on drug and alcohol abuse to Illinois State students. The answer, of course, is no. "They put themselves in a position where they were constantly affecting their ability to learn."

The new regulations have only been in place for a few years at Illinois State, but anecdotal evidence suggests they're making an impact. "It's registering with students that we're serious," Olshak says.

State laws vary widely when it comes to drugs, in part due to different thresholds that distinguish between citations and misdemeanors, and between misdemeanors and felonies. The possession of 24 grams of pot in one state might merit a civil citation and a $100 fine. Possession of the exact same amount in another state, where the threshold is 20 grams, can result in a felony charge, a five-year prison sentence, and a $5,000 fine. First-time violators at the lowest level who do not commit an aggravating crime (like assault) at the time of their arrest are more likely to receive minimum sanctions, although judges have the leeway to exercise their own discretion. Regardless, would you ever want to be in a predicament where a five-year prison sentence for drug possession is even a remote possibility?

Paul Campbell has some friends who ended up in such a position. They were traveling through Texas while on the way to visit one of the student's homes. They were pulled over for running a stoplight and subsequently arrested for possession of illegal drugs, Paul explains. "In Texas the drug laws are extremely tough, and now they are serving three years' probation. It very nearly ruined their lives. Now they have this on their record and won't be able to get it off."

Here are a few more examples of how drug use can destroy one's college career:

- ✓ Many scholarships have character stipulations, meaning the scholarship funding can be rescinded if the recipient receives any sanctions for drug use.
- ✓ Athletic teams may suspend or dismiss students who either test positive for drugs or who are caught using them. Scholarship athletes may lose their scholarships, as well.
- ✓ It shouldn't need to be stated, but we'll point it out anyway: Driving while under the influence of drugs could result in far worse than an arrest or an inadvertent fender-bender. A charge of criminally negligent homicide will mean that getting kicked out of school would be the smallest problem that needs to be dealt with. Unfortunately, many young people who are aware of the dangers of drunk driving wrongly think they can smoke marijuana and still get behind the wheel. That misconception can be fatal. "Marijuana does not 'heighten' your senses, rather it alters them," says Dr. Sharon Levy.

How can I handle the pressure I might feel to try drugs?

When you read the word "pressure" above, you probably leaped straight to the stereotypical image that's been infused in your mind since middle school—the idea that your friends are standing in a semicircle, forcing you to engage in some conformist activity that doesn't really represent who you are.

That's one kind of pressure, to be sure, but now is a good time to file that image in the back of your mind, and consider another kind of pressure that can be equally overwhelming: pressure from within.

Most students seem to understand that college is a time to be independent and do what they want to do, for their own sake. As a result, many students interviewed say they're very comfortable responding "no" if someone offers them a substance they're not interested in. And nine times out of ten, the person offering backs off. "Peers would never hassle you or make fun because you don't smoke weed—they would merely offer you a hit if you are sitting there," says Ben Sarle (University of Vermont, Class of 2006).

Instead of facing pressure from your friends, the pressure can mount internally to try things that others are doing. In other words, their laughter among themselves and camaraderie as they pass around a substance—with no scorn or ridicule directed at you—can be the college-level version of peer pressure.

> *"I don't understand people who use peer pressure as an excuse—a person has to be a real coward to let a couple of people force them into doing something they don't want to do. You're responsible for your own actions, so don't use the lame, 'I was pressured to do it.'"*
>
> —Grace Choe, University of Southern California, Class of 2005

"For the most part, you aren't going to feel pressure to light up like the television public service announcements would want you to think," says Ben. "In college, a typical pressure I experienced would be that I might walk into a room where a few of my friends are passing a bong around and ordering way too much [pizza], and I might want to take part."

Keep in mind that if you refuse an offer of drugs, it's doubtful you'll be alone. And if you are the only one in your group not using drugs regularly, instead of contemplating joining them, perhaps you should reconsider whom you're hanging out with.

"Not 'everyone' is doing it," says Kevin McPherson of the University of Texas at Austin. "I've never done drugs and I know a lot of people who haven't. I know some people who smoke weed all the time. Have bad things happened to them? Not really, but their grades slip and they just sit around all day, not doing anything but smoking—not really something to aspire to."

The people who steer clear of drugs, however, are not always nearby when you need them. Rebekah Lee (Rutgers University, Class of 2007) says a friend of hers was ostracized by her floormates because she neither drank nor smoked pot. "She survived," reports Rebecca, who urges students in the same situation to stick to their principles and stick with their likeminded friends. "It's much easier to resist pressure when you have a few friends who feel the way you do. Don't think that giving in and partaking in something that goes against who you are will make things easier."

Grace Choe of Southern Cal urges students to rely on their collegiate sense of independence when turning down drugs. She also suggests being forceful when turning down an offer to partake in drug use. A timid response, she says, can send mixed signals that you really might just need your arm twisted: "Don't say it in a passive voice, like 'Oh . . . nooo . . . it's ooookay.' Rather, just say, 'No thanks, it's not really my thing.'"

12

Rape

> *We once broke down a door to get our friend out of a room we knew she was in with a guy. She was very, very drunk and wasn't really coherent. We didn't care if that guy got mad. We just wanted our friend out of there in case anything happened.*
>
> —Samantha Del Priore, Seton Hall University, Class of 2006

Kate Dieringer woke up late one September night her freshman year, in a mental and physical fog, in the apartment of a fellow student. She couldn't move; he was having sex with her.

"I'm lying there, his doll. His heavy torso on me, pressing into my abdomen, moving back and forth. I am paralyzed and confused. I try to sit up. His weight pushes me back to the bed. He is completely naked. He is on top of me. I push on his shoulders, and he ignores me."

Kate (Georgetown University, Class of 2005) wrote the words above in an article titled "The Girl Who Whimpered Rape" in the *Georgetown Voice*. In it, she writes that she was drugged by the male student who separated her from her friends at a gathering and then sexually assaulted her in his apartment:

"All I can do is watch what is slowly coming to a reality in my head. I pitifully say, 'No.' I push his shoulders. 'No!' He stays inside of me. All I can say is 'No.' I don't know if we are still in the apartment that I think we came into, however long ago. I see what's happening to me. I'm being raped, and I don't know what to do. I regain all mobility, and I try to kick my legs. My eyelids are heavy and I don't have enough power to get up. 'No!' and my eyes start to tear up. I finally kick him off and jump up."

His response, according to Kate's account: "Fine, be a stupid freshman bitch."

Kate emerged from the assault as a very public voice for rape victims. But her path to justice was marked in many places by doubt and denial where she hoped to find support and encouragement, she has said. She has explained that following the incident, after months of therapy, frequent spontaneous bursts of tears, and withdrawal from the usual joys of college life, she decided to report it to campus officials—to ensure the same thing doesn't happen again to someone else.

Kate has stated that she found layer on top of layer of a system that seemed more intent on protecting the accused assailant than protecting other female students or even showing sensitivity to her. Public safety officers were skeptical, Georgetown's Office of Student Conduct "belittled and harassed me to tears," and college president John J. DeGioia would not meet with her parents, according to Kate.

At the conclusion of an exhaustive hearing process, in the spring of 2002, a panel of Georgetown students and faculty expelled the male student, according to published reports about the incident. But he appealed, and the sanctions were reduced to a one-year suspension. In an unusual twist, though, Georgetown officials told Kate she could not learn the case's outcome unless she signed a confidentiality agreement, promising to share details only with her parents and one close adviser.

Kate, joined by the campus-safety watchdog group Security on Campus, Inc., filed a complaint about the disclosure policy with the U.S. Department of Education. In the summer of 2004, the department told Georgetown that the policy violated federal campus crime laws. As a result of the ruling and Kate's determination, colleges must now be more open about sharing the outcomes of such cases—something many schools, unfortunately, would prefer to keep quiet.

Georgetown officials have maintained that the university handled the case fairly and was acting in good faith, with the intent of protecting the privacy of both students. They have pointed out that the university's Student Disciplinary System is not run like a criminal court, nor is it intended to function as one. Georgetown was not fined by the government—only told that it must change its ways.

Kate's case illustrates the despicable nature of rape—a crime committed by individuals who prey on victims who are weaker or who suffer from diminished capacity. Education is perhaps the best weapon against this bane. It can help potential assailants, such as otherwise all-American college-age men, realize they must absolutely be sure that sex is 100 percent mutually agreed upon. It can help potential victims avoid the circumstances that make rape more likely to happen. And it can also help third parties know that there are times when they must intervene.

This first part of this chapter focuses on what all students should know about rape, particularly its prevalence on campus and the routine circumstances that breed it. The latter part addresses the many ways that victims and their supporters can respond after an attack.

What do I need to know about rape on campus?

The question above may not appear to relate to an actual decision. But it does: It relates to a decision to stick your head in the sand about a critical issue, or to become informed and possibly head off such an attack, either on yourself or involving someone you know.

Perhaps the most important thing to know about campus rape is that it happens. It happens to regular college students who think they're safe when they end up in the wrong circumstances with the wrong person. And the rapists are often students who would otherwise be considered trustworthy.

The term "date rape" is often applied to these attacks, because the victim is highly likely to know her assailant. But the term is a misnomer. The "rape" part is right. The "date" part isn't. It's not something that typically follows a dinner-and-a-movie date. It's much more likely to happen when a group of people are consuming alcohol or drugs, and two people—who may have only gotten to know each other that evening—pair off.

Only when they're in a bedroom together might things start to go gravely wrong. It comes down to consent. The woman, who typically has a significantly lower tolerance for alcohol and drugs than a man, might become incoherent or otherwise incapacitated, even if she doesn't totally pass out. In short, she cannot decide for herself whether to have sex. The issue of consent is central—that woman is no different in the eyes of the law than an 8-year-old child or a comatose patient, both of whom cannot under any circumstances be considered to consent to sexual contact. If the man proceeds to have sex with her, it's not enough that she didn't say "no." Since she physically lacked the ability to consent, it's a clear case of rape.

"It is very important for women who are entering college to be aware of the risks in being taken advantage of or raped while you or he is under the influence," says Catherine Bell (University of Kansas, Class of 2004), who points out that college women are vulnerable in large part due to the prevalence of heavy drinking on campus.

Statistics show that rape is a serious issue on college campuses.

Between one-fifth and one-quarter of college women who attend school for five years will either be raped or be the target of an attempted rape, according to "The Sexual Victimization of College Women," a 2000 research report prepared for the U.S. Department of Justice by Bonnie S. Fisher, Francis T. Cullen, and Michael G. Turner. Most cases occur, they report, when college women are alone with a man they know, at night, in a residence such as a dorm room. They also found that "frequently drinking enough to get drunk" was a consistent trait of the sexual assault victims.

"The Sexual Victimization of College Women" researchers interviewed more than 4,000 female college students and asked them about their experiences during the current school year. They found that 2.8 percent had experienced either a completed rape (1.7 percent) or an attempted rape (1.1 percent) since the beginning of the school year, which worked out to an average period of 6.91 months (depending on when they actually took the survey). The 2.8 percent

A Little-Known Fact About College Rape

Female freshmen face the greatest risk of being raped between the start of college and Thanksgiving Break, according to a report delivered on the Web site factsontap.com, produced by the American Council for Drug Education and the Children of Alcoholics Foundation. With regard to alcohol, such students might be considered vulnerable during that time because they may:

- ✓ wrongly believe that all students drink excessively and feel that they must, too
- ✓ don't know how much alcohol they can handle, and may not find out until they've gone past that limit
- ✓ fail to understand how heavy drinking can render students oblivious, unconscious, or susceptible to grave harm
- ✓ feel a false sense of security when drinking with fellow students who may themselves be impaired and not in a position to be trustworthy

These factors can form a tragic mixture when combined with a male student—often one who's had too much to drink, himself—intent on having sex.

victimization figure over nearly seven months was then projected to a full-year rate of 4.9 percent. To arrive at their final figures, researchers then took this rate and multiplied it by the typical number of years it takes students to complete school—four or five.

The statistics may not be perfect, the authors say. When the full-year rates were projected forward for the "college career" rate, for example, they didn't take into account the conditions students face during the summer, when they're usually not at school. And, of course, some students take more, or less, time to graduate. Regardless, "The Sexual Victimization of College Women" clearly shows that sexual assault on campus is not a rare, isolated problem.

A Coaster Can Help

Drink Safe Technology, an Alabama-based company, manufactures inexpensive coasters and "test strips" that can detect whether a drink is tainted. Students place a drop of the drink on two sections of the coaster or strip, rub it, then wait until it dries. If either circle changes to a dark-blue color, the drink is bad, according to the company.

The research also points out that most victims know their attackers. "For both completed and attempted rapes, about 9 in 10 offenders were known to the victim," the report states. "Most often, a boyfriend, ex-boyfriend, classmate, friend, acquaintance, or co-worker sexually victimized the women. College professors were not identified as committing any rapes or sexual coercions, but they were cited as the offender in a low percentage of cases involving unwanted sexual contact."

Samantha Del Priore (Seton Hall University, Class of 2006) says she's mindful that sexual assault can happen. "It's not something that you just hear about," says Samantha, whose quote at the very top of this chapter shows how seriously she takes the matter. When your mom tells you not to leave your drink somewhere at a party and then come back to it, she's right. I haven't had any experiences with it, but I do know that it happens and you have to be very careful."

She and her friends look out for each other whenever they go to parties. "We never leave someone there alone," she says. "We all bring our cellphones just in case."

Lindsay Haymes (Southwest Missouri State University, Class of 2006) also urges caution when going out. "Drinking and hanging out with men you don't know isn't really safe, because you could be taken advantage of," says Lindsay.

Stalking is another campus crime that both genders need to be aware of. More than 13 percent of participants in "The Sexual Victimization of College Women" study reported being stalked since the start of the school year (again, an average of about 6.91 months, based on when the survey was taken). The incidents most

Avoiding Campus Rape

How can you avoid being any part of a campus rape? Here are some commonly advised suggestions that will greatly reduce the risk:

✓ Do not become intoxicated, either by alcohol or other drugs. Once you lose your ability to reason, or consent, bad things can happen. Note: It's essential to always point out—and we won't miss the opportunity here—that of course no one ever "asks" to be raped. But the reality that it occurs so frequently when victims are drunk or high must be pointed out. It's the same logic as cautioning someone not to wear flashy jewelry when walking through a dark alley on the wrong side of town.

✓ Always stay with friends you can trust. Make a pact that you will look out for each other and never allow an intoxicated member of your group to leave with someone who cannot be trusted.

✓ Watch your drink carefully so that no one can spike it with alcohol or another drug. Never leave your drink unattended. Avoid batches of punch and similar concoctions where you can never be sure of the contents. Consider drinking only bottled beverages that you opened yourself or clearly observed being opened. So-called "date-rape" drugs such as Rohypnol, Gamma Hydroxy Butyrate, and Ketamine Hydrochloride are odorless and tasteless—even when slipped into water—and can render a person incapable of consenting to sex. Maintaining complete control over what you drink is the only way to avoid these drugs.

✓ Take advantage of emergency "blue-light" telephones that dot many college campuses. Always err on the side of playing it safe. If you think you're being followed, or that you might pass out, or even if you're simply scared and afraid to cross campus by yourself late at night, pick up the phone under the illuminated blue light. It will typically provide an automatic link to campus security. The officers are trained to respond promptly and provide assistance to any student in distress. Once on the line, do not understate or play down your fears.

✓ Trust your internal instincts and get out of any situation the moment you realize it has the potential to go wrong. If you realize you probably shouldn't have gone back to someone's room, at 3 a.m., for example, just walk out immediately. Don't say you're leaving. Just leave. It may be easier to do so at that point than if you wait until the lights are out and you're both on a bed together.

frequently included the victims being telephoned (77.7 percent), having an offender waiting outside or inside places (47.9 percent), being watched from afar (44 percent), being followed (42 percent), being sent letters (30.7 percent), and being e-mailed (24.7 percent). Almost two-thirds said they were stalked at least two to six times a week. The stalkers were most frequently a boyfriend or ex-boyfriend (42.5 percent), classmate (24.5 percent), acquaintance (10.3 percent), friend (5.6 percent), or co-worker (5.6 percent), the study states.

The study's authors note that their definition of stalking is broader than that of many state statutes, which require a stated threat of physical harm. Using that definition, 1.96 percent of the sample would be considered stalking victims.

How do I get help if I am the victim of a sexual assault?

The first hours after a sexual assault are critical—it's the time when victims may be most traumatized, although it may take days or weeks before the full magnitude hits some students. But it's also the time when victims are likely to remember the most significant details of the attack, and when critical evidence can be collected and analyzed. It may be more difficult to establish a case if there is a delay in reporting the crime. With this in mind, campus security officials and victims' advocates recommend taking the following actions after an attack:

- ✓ **Go to a safe place.** Whether or not you use the blue-light phones, go to a business such as a pizzeria, or enter any campus building. Go somewhere public where you won't be further harmed.
- ✓ **Do not shower or clean yourself in any way.** Doing so may remove the evidence that could send your assailant to prison.
- ✓ **Get medical attention for all injuries.** Only a trained professional can administer a Rape Kit Exam, to collect forensic evidence from the assault. Tests will also be administered for sexually transmitted diseases and pregnancy, although follow-up tests will also be needed.
- ✓ **Contact the police.** Campus police will investigate the crime on the university's behalf and possibly serve as a liaison to city or county police. City or county police will investigate the crime with a goal of arresting the rapist. They may also target the conditions that lead to the rape, such as a bar or a fraternity that allowed minors to drink.
- ✓ **Tell your parents and a trusted friend.** Their support can make a huge difference at this painful time. You may also wish to inform your Resident Adviser, who can help you contact other sources of assistance.
- ✓ **Contact the women's center, campus support services, or the equivalent at your school.** They can provide an advocate who will stay with you every step of the way, from police interviews to medical exams, to the filing of criminal charges.
- ✓ **Seek counseling or support.** Your college should be able to provide you with a counselor who can help you through the crisis.

There may possibly be overlap among services provided by some of the above sources, but each has a strength that victims should not hesitate to avail themselves of. In addition, although all of the above should provide professional, compassionate assistance, it's possible that you'll be in touch with someone at some point who doesn't take your concern seriously, as Kate Dieringer found out. If that's the case, demand more professional assistance. Have an advocate at your side during all interactions with authorities. Do not let anyone's ignorance deter you from getting the help you deserve.

The resources for sexual assault victims vary from school to school, but in all cases, your college either has trained professionals on hand or has direct access to ones who can help you through the ordeal.

Colleges aim to be particularly sensitive about rape. Part of it stems from informed and enlightened students who have pressured schools to institute safety measures such as blue-light phone systems. And part of it comes from leaders at schools who take a proactive approach to such crimes. Boise State University in Idaho, for example, spells out its sexual assault response policy to students with the following guarantee of sensitive, quality assistance:

Boise State University Sexual Assault Response Policy

We will meet with you privately or at a place of your choice to file a complaint report.

We will not release your name to the public or to the press. Crime statistics and incidents are made public record.

Our officers will not prejudge you, and you will not be blamed for what occurred.

We will treat you and your particular case with courtesy, sensitivity, dignity, understanding, and professionalism.

If you have a preference for either a female or male officer, we will do our best to accommodate your request.

We will assist you in receiving hospital, medical, counseling, and other support services that are available.

We will fully investigate your case, and will help you to achieve the best outcome. This may involve the arrest and full prosecution of the suspect(s). You will be kept informed of the progress of the investigation and/or prosecution.

We will consider your case seriously regardless of your gender, sexual orientation, and regardless of the gender or sexual orientation of the suspect(s).

—Reprinted by permission of Boise State University

You should expect your school to take an approach that is similar to the one promised by Boise State. Activism-minded students might consider inquiring about the policy toward sexual-assault victims at their own school, and pressing for the development of one if it doesn't already exist.

What should I consider when deciding whether to file charges?

Perhaps the biggest decision faced by victims of sexual assault is whether to file a report with campus or city police, and whether to cooperate in the prosecution of a suspect. While proceeding with the process and bringing the attacker to justice may seem like the obvious choice, many women decline to pursue legal remedies because they fear being victimized again.

"The Sexual Victimization of College Women" reports that less than 5 percent of the self-identified victims of rape or attempted rape in its study filed a report with police. Two-thirds did tell someone else about the incident, but it was most often a friend, not a family member or college representative. The victims, according to the report, gave the following reasons for declining:

- ✓ They did not see the incidents as harmful or important enough to merit notifying authorities.
- ✓ They do not want family members or acquaintances to know about the incident. (Though not specifically cited in the study, rape victims are often afraid of the media coverage that will follow the filing of a report.)

- ✓ They are afraid that there will not be enough evidence that the attack happened. They are also concerned that they'll be treated with hostility by police, or that authorities will not take the matter seriously.
- ✓ They fear reprisals from their assailant.

Kate Dieringer's case shows why some women don't want to get involved, but it also shows why other women press onward. Some victims may want so badly to put the rape behind them that they decline any suggestion that they notify authorities. It's not easy to find Kate's strength to confront her alleged assailant, cope with the skeptics, and continue with college to graduate on time. But on the other hand, Kate's perseverance resulted in a major victory, one with nationwide consequences.

The main problem with cutting off legal remedies quickly after a rape is that it may be more difficult, although by no means impossible, to press charges later on. From a police perspective, it's best to collect all information and evidence immediately after the crime has been committed. As time passes, physical evidence is destroyed or deteriorates, and exact details—such as a precise timeline of events—may fade from memory.

The decision of how to proceed in these cases is, clearly, intensely personal. It is best made based on factors unique to each case, and made in consultation with people who have the victim's individual interests foremost in mind.

13

Special Situations

> *College life can be rocky and full of uncertainty. It is just harder if you try to tackle things alone.*
>
> —Melissa Hernandez, Colby College, Class of 2005

Whether you're a straight-A, never-drink-or-smoke, yes-ma'am kind of student or one who's just getting by, some measure of trouble is likely to find you at some point in your college career. You may be the one in trouble, or it could be a friend of yours who's caught in a tight situation. Whether you're dealing with severe depression or your roommate has just used her one phone call to tell you she's in the county jail on pot-possession charges, the decisions made in these moments of crisis can have lasting implications.

In this chapter, students share how they've handled their bouts with tough times, ranging from personal to legal confrontations, and a legal expert offers guidance that may be useful if you ever have to face the police.

How do I get help if I have some sort of problem?

It's easy to complain about college: It's expensive, for starters. Those big lecture classes don't appear to be the best way to learn. And the food's not always so great. But one area where colleges tend to succeed is in making help available to students. Schools offer professional help for almost any problem imaginable, from poor study habits to depression to substance abuse.

Help is always available, no matter how serious the problem. However, the schools can't always find students in need. Unless a friend or college official reports your warning signs, the only way to get help is to take the initiative to call up or show up and ask for it.

"Knowing about the college's resources for help is a vital thing," says Colby College student Melissa Hernandez (Class of 2005), "especially on those nights where you're lying in bed, huddled in the darkness, letting your thoughts rattle deep into the late hours, praying . . . for guidance."

Melissa experienced some of those nights and didn't seek help at first; she almost dropped out of college as a result. As a Puerto Rican female from the New York City borough of Staten Island, she initially felt a sense of shame at the Maine college, located in a part of the nation not known for ethnic diversity. "Because I was Puerto Rican, if an alarm would go off in a store, they'd look at me, they'd question me. Who could I tell that to? 'Victim' wasn't a word that I would apply to myself, but I sure felt like one. Lots of little instances would occur in my social life, some based on race, some my gender, but because I didn't know who to talk to about those hurts, I considered leaving the school."

She took some time off from school, and says she was able to defeat some of those feelings with the help of several connections she made at Colby. "I learned that living at college is about knowing when to ask for help," she says with appreciation for those willing to assist at a moment's notice, from professionals to advisers to classmates. "Because at night, when you're in your dorm, sometimes nothing's better than knowing you can call somebody if you need to."

Those who want to find help on their own can contact their college's office of student services or health center. Resident advisers are also a great place to start—they're trained to point students in the right direction.

"Or, if the subject is personal, go online and utilize your college Web site to find the services available to you," advises Rebekah Lee (Rutgers University, Class of 2007). She also urges students not to feel alone: "Problems you will have will not be unique to you—even if it seems like you are the only one adjusting [or] having

A Few Words About Suicide

Some student concerns demand immediate help. Suicide is at the top of the list. It's the second-leading cause of death among college students (after accidents), according to the Jed Foundation, a nonprofit foundation formed in 2000 by the parents of a college student who committed suicide in 1998.

The foundation works with colleges on suicide-prevention programs. It urges students to watch for signs of depression, such as sadness or anxiety; feelings of guilt, helplessness, or hopelessness; trouble eating or sleeping; withdrawing from friends and/or social activities; loss of interest in hobbies, work, school; increased use of alcohol or drugs; anger; or excessive irritability or impulsivity. The foundation's Web site, www.jedfoundation.org, also notes four specific signs of potential suicide:

- ✓ Talking openly about committing suicide
- ✓ Talking indirectly about "wanting out" or "ending it all"
- ✓ Taking unnecessary or life-threatening risks
- ✓ Giving away personal possessions

The Jed Foundation has created a Web site, www.ulifeline.com, packed with information and resources about the subject, especially for college students. It recommends The National Hopeline Network—1-800-SUICIDE or 1-800-784-2433—through which counselors are available 24 hours a day.

trouble with grades . . . there will be many people feeling just as apprehensive as you."

Even if a problem is not health-related, it pays to contact those who can ameliorate it. If you're bothered, for example, about a financial issue with your school, don't let it fester—contact the appropriate office, says Lindsay Haymes (Southwest Missouri State University, Class of 2006). "Learn early on at least the different offices on your campus, so if you have a problem you have a general idea where to start," she recommends.

Similarly, if academics are giving you trouble, contact your professor. Most will be sympathetic to students who take the time to ask politely for personal help.

Adam Abelkop (Wake Forest University Class of 2007) says most of his professors would like nothing more than to help him succeed. "You just can't be afraid to go into their offices during office hours and talk—they're just people trying to make a living."

Whoever you talk to, don't be afraid to seek help. "I've wandered around academic buildings in a fog because I didn't have enough courage to speak away the hurt," says Melissa Hernandez. "People are there to listen. If you like a particular dean or professor, go to them. It's whoever you feel comfortable with."

When do I get involved in my friend's problems?

University of Vermont student Ben Sarle (Class of 2006) recalls a college friend of his who had a unique problem that was "out of character" for him. (The problem is not described here because it could identify the friend.) After being in touch with the friend's mother, Ben and other close friends let their pal know that they were aware of what was going on. They offered their support and encouragement—and in this case, it was enough to make a difference.

"He knew we were aware and concerned, and even though he didn't say anything at the time, he has told us recently that it helped him to know that we cared about him enough to bring it up," says Ben. "Better to get involved than to be sorry. Get involved in your friend's problems if you think it could harm them or somebody else."

Good friends have an obligation to get involved if a friend's problem threatens their health or well-being.

"What kind of best friend are you if you do not get involved with their problems?" asks Kim Miller (College of William and Mary, Class of 2005). She qualifies her response, though, by pointing out that getting involved "does not mean being a busybody and a nosy friend." Instead, it means listening, understanding, and respecting. It also involves knowing when to yield to a professional, and helping your friend get in touch with such assistance.

Students might feel overwhelmed when they confront a friend's crisis. That's why it's important that they don't burden themselves with the responsibility of solving the problem. "Let her know how much you care for her, and that you're not trying to do her mom's job," says Catherine Anne Bennion (Brigham Young University, Class of 2007).

Erica Lemansky (Brandeis Univesity, Class of 2005) concurs, pointing out that the more dangerous the situation, the greater the urgency of getting involved. Among the most dire crises: eating disorders, overly depressive behavior, alcohol or drug abuse, repetitive illnesses, and suicide (addressed immediately above this section). "When your friend's health or safety is in danger, it is definitely appropriate for you to get involved," she says. She suggests confronting your friend about the situation and giving her a chance to get help, and then monitoring the situation carefully. "If all else fails, seek help from a resident adviser, peer counseling group, or staff member of your university."

> *"If you have a friend who is going through a tough time, or is making some bad decisions, you could be the only thing between them and the 'mistake of a lifetime.'"*
>
> —Lindsay Haymes, Southwest Missouri State University, Class of 2006

One student at a university in the east explains that he got involved with his girlfriend's depression, and is glad he did. At first, he shared his concern with his own friends, but he then sought the guidance of his parents as well as university administrators. All of them proved instrumental in getting his girlfriend some help.

"There is no need to hide from anyone, especially your parents, when you have a problem or are dealing with a problem that is not even really yours," says the student, a member of his Class of 2007.

What should I do if I'm pulled over by the police?

Winter Park, Florida, is typical of many college towns. The low-crime city, located near Orlando in Central Florida, is home to about 25,000 residents, as well as Rollins College. "Aloma [Avenue], the main road to school, is an especially notorious speed trap" with traffic cops who are numerous and aggressive, says Rollins student Selena Moshell, who's paid fines between $100 and $150 for going 10 to 15 mph over the speed limit.

Similar spots exist on or near college campuses nationwide. And while there are occasions when students receive a summons unfairly, it's more likely that the police had a good reason to make the traffic stop. When this happens, students say the best strategy is to play it straight.

"Tell the truth and appeal to their sympathy," says Erick M. Bousman of the University of South Carolina's Class of 2006. "More importantly, avoid being pulled over in the first place."

Lauren Hardgrove (Ohio University, Class of 2005) agrees. She says cops know when students are lying, so rather than insult them with outlandish excuses or explanations, try cooperating—and maybe you will get off with a warning. Lauren offers this advice based on two traffic tickets she's received. Although she was honest, she admits to being less than pleasant, and realizes that politeness might be the best way to go.

John Andersen (University of Missouri–Columbia, Class of 2007) suggests not panicking when you see the police lights in the rear-view mirror, regardless of whether you committed an infraction. "One night I was on the way home from my girlfriend's around midnight when I was pulled over by three state police cars at the same time," he recalls. "It turned out that they were just looking for a stolen car similar to mine and had pulled me over because I crossed the 'fog line'—that white line on the outside of the road. I received no citation and the officer was very apologetic."

Going to Traffic Violation Court

The place to argue your case is in court, and while getting completely cleared is unlikely, you may get your fine reduced. Your best hope is that the officer fails to show up, in which case the ticket may be dismissed.

Selena Moshell of Rollins College is convinced that it's not worth trying to fight your way out of a ticket with a traffic cop: "It has never, and will never, work for me, I'm convinced." Disputing one ticket in court—because the stop sign was obscured—did pay off, however. The judge dismissed the ticket not because of her argument, but because the officer failed to show up.

If you do go to court, make sure you keep your appointment, suggests Grace Choe (University of Southern California, Class of 2005), or your fine could multiply. If you can't attend the hearing, don't just pull a "no show"—ask for a one-time adjournment.

If you disagree with the ticket you're about to receive, you might want to try politely explaining your point of view, but don't press the matter if you're rebuffed. Sensing your determination to prevail, the officer might seek to bolster his case by issuing a second summons for failure to wear a seatbelt or a secondary infraction, if it's warranted.

University of Louisville student Lisa Hall (Class of 2004) was once pulled over for running a red light during a heavy rainstorm. It was close, she admits, but she feared that if she jammed on the brakes, she'd slide through the intersection and possibly cause a collision. "I tried to explain this to the officer, and he said, 'Well, if you weren't going so fast, you wouldn't have had to worry about that,'" remembers Lisa. "Anyway, it's no use to argue. You won't win."

Grace Choe has had her share of moving violations. Her experiences illustrate a few points that all drivers, not just those in college, should be mindful of:

✓ **The cops are frequently looking, even if you think they're not.** ("I was stuck in a bunch of 'no left-turn' lanes, so I just made the illegal turn . . . I didn't even look behind me to see that a black-and-white was right behind me.")

✓ **It doesn't matter if traffic is light—you may still receive a summons if you speed.** (She was once cited for going 90 mph in a 65 mph zone on the open road in Kansas.)

✓ **Charm doesn't always work.** ("I was going to flash the cop a cute smile until I saw a female blonde coming out of the patrol car and knew there was no way out.")

✓ **Having a lousy day doesn't mean that the cops will let you get away with making an illegal U-turn.** ("I had just quit my awful internship.")

If you're convicted of a traffic violation, you may have the opportunity to go to "traffic school" or the equivalent (that may, in fact, be part of your sentence, depending on the infraction). Depending on your insurance carrier, and your state's laws and penalties, traffic school can negate the worst part of the traffic ticket—the hike in your insurance rate.

Grace attests to the painful insurance spike. She owns a 2003 Toyota 4Runner, and pays a $1,050 premium every six months, she explains. "If I didn't have a ticket on my record, it would be $300 less . . . And it will take three years for it to be removed from my record—so doing the math, I will pay an additional $1,800 over a period of three years."

What should I do if I'm arrested or otherwise confronted by the police?

College students and cops sometimes mix about as well as beer and milk. The students are at a peak point in their lives where they're questioning authority. They tend to drink more than they should, with many using fake IDs to procure their spirits. And in many college towns, students are responsible for more than their share of calls to the police, ranging from noise complaints to vandalism, and from fights to sexual assault.

Despite the carefree atmosphere that prevails among many college students, they are not immune to the kinds of mistakes that can land them in legal trouble. Otherwise "good" students might go too far with a fraternity stunt and end up facing misdemeanor hazing charges. Someone else may be arrested after being caught with a forged driver's license. Another may face prison time because a fist fight resulted in serious injuries to the other party, as well as an assault charge.

While students may get into trouble for any number of reasons, alcohol is likely to be a factor, according to attorney Gary Sommer, who has provided counsel to hundreds of Syracuse University students in his years as director of its Student Legal Services. Many colleges provide free or low-cost legal services for students who need them.

"Fifty percent of everything we deal with is alcohol-related," he says, referring to incidents involving fake ID, underage drinking, fights, DWI, and even noisy parties that get out of hand. When it comes to DWI cases and fights, the potential penalties can be sky high because of the possibility of grave injury.

Fights almost always involve male students, and can usually be attributed to a potent combination of alcohol and testosterone. "You don't see women getting into fights too often," he points out.

One student he represented was involved in a fight, and hit the other guy over the head with a beer bottle. A total of 78 stitches were needed to close the wound, and his client faced felony assault charges.

In the vast majority of cases where there are no aggravating factors, Sommer says, students don't get the book thrown at them for first offenses. A typical scenario might include an ACD—an adjournment in contemplation of dismissal. A student might be required to do some community service, and then, if he stays out of trouble for a set period of time, the case is dropped.

But woe to those who slip up during that time—the old case will be revisited and stiffer penalties applied in addition to the sanctions arising from the second case.

For varying reasons, many students hesitate to tell their parents when they run into legal trouble. They're probably ashamed, on one level, and don't want to let them down. In other cases, they worry that their folks will come down hard on them—specifically by removing some financial support or a luxury such as the campus car.

What to Do If Confronted by Police

Regardless of your role in a troubling situation, you would be wise to follow some basic advice if confronted by police. Here are some tips from Gary Sommer, director of student legal services at Syracuse University:

1. "The first thing is to be polite. The second you get uppity, you get in a power struggle—you're going to lose that. Politeness is a good idea."
2. "Keep your mouth shut." Specifically, that involves not confessing to anything, because police will surely take note of any admission you make. "Most students feel intimidated" by the police, and as a result, they often volunteer more information than they should.
3. Know that you don't have to consent to a police search of your car or home without just cause. A cop knocking on your door might ask, "Mind if I look around?" While it's true that a refusal might arouse suspicion—especially if you have nothing to hide—you have plenty to lose if you allow the search and do have something to hide.
4. Not sure what to do? Contact an attorney. While all schools have different policies, if you contact your school's main telephone number or campus police, they should be able to help you connect with student legal services, or your school's equivalent.

Outside the heat of the moment, though, students usually realize that their parents can be their strongest advocates and best friends in these times of crisis, and that it's best to notify them if you're in trouble.

"I think the best thing to do would be let your parents know," says Tanner Sykes (Texas Tech University, Class of 2005). "Most students do not want to call their parents, but the fact of the matter is that they are going to find out one way or another. It's probably best to have them on your side from the beginning of the ordeal."

14

Grades

> *"I went to college and made sure to delegate my time wisely to encompass the many academic, social, and co-curricular activities that I would partake in. However, you need grades to make this experience truly work."*
>
> —Matthew Weber, Providence College, Class of 2006

Going to college is one of those life-changing experiences guaranteed to kick-start a conversation whenever you return home. Expect Mom, Dad, siblings, aunts, uncles, grandparents, cousins, and friends alike to interrogate you: "So, how's college?"

"Great" is always a safe response, but it avoids the real question lurking underneath: How are your grades? No matter how much fun you're having, grades are the biggest indicator of how it's really going. Depending on how strong they are, your grades can either validate your approach to college life or suggest that you need to make some changes.

This chapter focuses on the strategies students have taken to manage their grades—sometimes with success, sometimes without. They will tell how they've adjusted to the college grading system and how they've adapted their routines to get better grades. In other cases, they'll explain how their choices helped them balance their grades and a complete college experience.

How concerned should I be about grades?

Tiffany Rivera of Chantilly, Virginia, recalls heading out to Arizona State University for college when she was 17 years old. Like so many college campuses, Arizona State was brimming with places to party. She had an absolutely great time—"It's what it's cracked up to be," she says of college life in Tempe, where academics became an afterthought during her whirlwind first semester. "Needless to say, I didn't do so well."

Her first-semester GPA arrived with a thud: 1.47.

That includes an F in a class she took at night, but which she regularly blew off: "There's a lot more going on at 8 p.m. than microeconomics," she says, reflecting on the abundance of social opportunities. Her parents issued an ultimatum, which they were prepared to back up. "They said, 'Straighten up or get out.'"

She didn't straighten up, so she got out.

Tiffany returned home, where she first attended Northern Virginia Community College to earn her core credits. She then transferred to George Mason University, which she attends as a commuter student and where she'll receive her bachelor's degree in environmental science in 2005. There, she's taken a more serious and enthusiastic approach to her studies. It shows in her results. "I'm older and more focused" she says now.

Despite her struggles at Arizona State, Tiffany still considers her time there a "great experience." She clearly learned what she needed to do to succeed, and that academic success isn't likely with an "all-play-no-work" approach.

> *"Mom and Dad essentially buy a brand new car and drive it into a lake every year—that is your tuition. Make sure that you get something out of it—a good future and good grades."*
>
> —Nicholas Sauer, University of Denver, Class of 2005

Grades alone are hardly the only measure of success in college—but they do reflect how students handled the primary aspect of their collegiate experience.

It might help to look at the ideal situation, which is rarely achieved: perfect grades, heavy involvement in campus groups, and an active social life. For all but the brightest, most efficient, and hardest-working students, there simply are not enough hours in the week to do it all, especially for those also holding down a campus job.

So they tend to make small compromises with each of their goals. Such students are not "settling"—they're allocating their time in a way that lets them maximize their potential. Their choices might include:

- ✓ Limiting their campus involvements to a few groups they can devote a lot of time to. Those who join too many groups end up spreading themselves too thin, because they can't make meaningful contributions to all of them.
- ✓ Going out Friday and Saturday nights—but not Wednesdays and Thursdays, when pre-weekend action heats up at many schools.
- ✓ Working hard at academics, but not letting academics wipe out other important parts of college life. They might aim for a mixture of A's and B's—the rough equivalent of a highly respectable 3.5 GPA that's good enough for the dean's list at many schools. Even if the grades are evenly split among A's, B's, and C's, the GPA will still work out to a 3.0. (Try to avoid those C's, though.)

Most students seem to realize that an obsession with studying and grades—complete with pangs of misery over anything below an A—is an unhealthy way to approach college.

"Sometimes, I'll get worked up over a C that I got on an exam because I'm trying to boost my GPA in order to graduate with honors," says Rosanne Boyle (Providence College, Class of 2005). But she says she follows her mother's advice of not getting too stressed about such things. "Try your hardest in classes because that's what you're in college for, but don't stress yourself out to the point of exhaustion. Remember to have fun, too, or you'll always look back on college as that time when you studied too much and had no fun at all."

Kristen Watts (University of Texas at Austin, Class of 2006) agrees. She says she struggles sometimes to balance academics, her position on the rowing team, and her social life. "I've definitely mellowed a bit about my grades and realized that while they are important, the college experience as a whole is much more important," she says. "I work hard, and I also play hard." So while she manages a 3.7 GPA, she also makes the time to go dancing and swimming with her friends. Kristen also credits her parents for emphasizing the importance of a well-rounded college experience.

Similarly, Matthew Weber recalls chatting with his dad before heading off to Providence College for his studies. They discussed how grades are important, but also how college will nurture his personal growth, through his living arrangements and connections with friends, roommates, and classmates. "It's not just grades but the big picture," says Matthew, a member of the Class of 2006.

Students aiming to get into top-tier graduate schools, law schools, or medical schools usually need to make additional compromises in their college life, because a 3.0 GPA, or even a 3.5, may not be enough—despite a healthy mixture of extracurricular involvements.

Rebekah Lee (Rutgers University, Class of 2007) majors in biology (pre-medicine) and history. She recalls the halcyon days of high school, where she says relatively little effort was needed to earn a 3.85 GPA, even with a full slate of Advanced Placement courses. "In college—especially my pre-med classes—it isn't unusual for me to study 15 or 20 hours for one exam," says Rebekah. "It sounds scary, and it is a little bit, but you can adjust. It just takes time and effort on your part. Keep up your self-discipline, even though it can be hard, and you will be fine."

Laurie Quaife, a 2004 graduate of Kansas State University, recalls making lots of sacrifices to get the highest grades so that she'll be able to attend law school—something she plans to do after working a few years. "I had to be really good at managing my time, which meant that I had to be selective about hanging out with friends," she says. "I couldn't just drop everything and go whenever someone wanted to hang out. I did have time for a social life but I didn't have quite as active of a social life as some of my

More Reasons to Get Good Grades

If personal pride, graduate school ambitions, and the threat of Mom and Dad yanking their financial support aren't enough, there are still plenty of other reasons to pay close attention to grades in college:

- ✓ Students who have received scholarships or financial aid packages—either through private foundations, the government, or their college—usually must maintain solid grades or the funding may be rescinded. "I'm very concerned about my grades," says Samatha Del Priore (Seton Hall University, Class of 2006). "I always have been, but even more so now because I need to keep a 3.0 GPA to keep my scholarship."
- ✓ Membership in some university organizations, ranging from honor societies to university ambassadors, is contingent on a certain GPA level. In addition, many fraternities and sororities—always eager to shed their "Animal House" reputations—have higher academic standards than the colleges they're a part of. Those who don't keep up risk their status as a brother or sister in the house.
- ✓ You may change your mind midway through college and decide on a career path that demands higher grades—or won't accept mediocre grades. "I knew students who part-way through decided they wanted to attend law school but struggled with it because they hadn't taken their GPA seriously in the beginning," says Laurie Quaife of Kansas State University. "It's best to start out strong—that way you won't have any of your options limited in the future."
- ✓ If your academic struggles are related to your unhappiness at the school, poor grades will only make it more difficult to transfer to another school. At best, you'll be limited to schools with lower academic standards than the one you're attending now.

friends. It was tough sometimes to watch people around me have all of this free time to watch TV and socialize, but I knew it would pay off. It was well worth it and if I had college to do again, I wouldn't change that."

How can I adjust to the midterm/final grading scheme?

One look at a typical freshman class syllabus lays bare the reasons why many flounder during their first semester. It's a time when freshmen are possibly taking several large, lecture-style classes, where attendance is not counted, and where the only assignment for September may be the class reading list. It's possible that only one or two of their classes, such as freshman English, require writing assignments or problem-solving homework in the first few weeks.

Then October strikes, like a tidal wave, in the form of midterm exams.

Some students sink, while others swim.

Students may face four or five midterms—and possibly well more than 1,000 pages to not only read, but to understand. By the time the storm subsides, the damage has been done—and clean college slates are washed away in a sea of red ink.

Large introductory undergraduate courses are most likely to follow the midterm/final grading scheme, where a midterm and final exam account for one's entire course grade. Some lecture-based courses might include a paper as an additional requirement, thus decreasing the weight of the exams, while others will take a portion of the grade from work done in discussion or recitation groups. But midterms and finals will always elicit so much student intensity because they can make or break a class grade in a one- or two-hour period.

In October, it's easy to spot the students who did their reading on those warm sunny September days. They're the ones who aren't stressing out, whose routines haven't changed, and who'll more often then not get the better grades.

Students say it's much tougher to play catch-up at these times than it is to study consistently throughout the semester. And they caution against underestimating the difficulty level of any class.

"The classes you think are easy and you end up not going to—those are the ones you end up doing the worst in," says Jake Liefer (University of Pittsburgh, Class of 2006).

Jake cited a statistics course he took in spring 2004 in which he received a C. "I thought I'd get an A," he says. But a slow start doomed his chances for a top grade. He realized he was in trouble by March. "I was already too far behind. You know that if you studied two hours a week, it wouldn't have been difficult at all."

Simply going to class and keeping up with the readings is a huge step in the right direction with any class, says Stephanie Yeager (University of Delaware, Class of 2006). "You could read 300 pages but you'll only be tested on 60."

> *"On your first day of class, when you look down at your course syllabus and see the words 'midterm: 45 percent, final: 45 percent, participation: 10 percent,' try not to freak out, because I did and it was not worth it. It is difficult to come to the realization that your entire class grade could ride on one test. But once you snap back to reality you can form your own study schedule."*
>
> —Alyssa Limberakis, Syracuse University, Class of 2006

Although even the best students struggle when faced with multiple exams in the same week, the best way to succeed in a class that heavily weights midterms and finals is to start preparing for those exams on the first day of class. "Create a schedule for yourself to work on that class in pieces," suggests Laurie Quaife. "You don't want to wait until the week of the midterm to do all of the reading. You will want the week of the midterm to be for review."

Alyssa Limberakis takes that approach at Syracuse. If she comes across something that she doesn't fully understand, that gives her the time to either ask the professor about it or confer with a classmate—a luxury procrastinators don't have.

Alan Tannenwald (Brandeis University, Class of 2005) also spreads his reading assignments out over the course of the semester, and works to identify the broad themes and key ideas that tend to surface on exams. He suggests typing up your notes to make a study guide; the act of writing serves to reinforce your knowledge. "I find this has worked for me for many types of courses, from philosophy to history," Alan says.

What adjustments should I consider after receiving my grades?

Are you a numbers person? If so, you know you can spend hours calculating how your grades might turn out. You know that an A and C is the equivalent of 2 B's, for example. Or that two B's and two A's will give you a strong 3.5 grade-point average.

All the guessing and projecting comes to a halt when first-semester grades are posted. And you don't have to be a numbers person to know if the letters spell good news or bad news. Those first-semester grades set the tone for how you'll approach subsequent semesters—you'll either work to maintain good grades, or you'll be in catch-up mode.

Catch-up mode is no fun.

"I had a friend who ended his first year with a GPA around a 1.0," says Adam Ritton (Creighton University, Class of 2007). "It took him until the second semester of his junior year to bring it up over a 3.0." One lesson to be learned, Adam says, is that it's not impossible to raise a lousy GPA. Indeed, with a GPA that low, a student must show immediate improvement or face dismissal at most colleges.

"It is not impossible to raise your GPA a few points, but it does require you to act early," Adam Ritton says. "On the other hand, sustaining a good GPA gets easier with time." He points out that those who maintain strong GPAs can actually "afford" the impact of an occasional lower-than-hoped-for grade.

How? A single C, for example, barely registers on the transcript of a first-semester junior with a 3.2 cumulative GPA—it would drop her index to about a 3.15. All those other good grades over the

> **The GPA Numbers Game**
>
> These scenarios are typical of what many students face. In each case, the value of starting off strong freshman year is clear:
>
> ✓ You get a 2.5 GPA your first semester, which is equal to an even mixture of B's and C's. In order to raise your overall GPA to a 3.0 after your first year, you'll need to get a 3.5—an even mixture of A's and B's—in the second semester.
>
> ✓ Your first-year GPA is a 3.5, but you take on too many outside challenges the first semester of sophomore year and get a 2.6 GPA, so your cumulative GPA dips to 3.2. The drop was cushioned by the strong freshman year.
>
> ✓ After three years, you have a 2.8 GPA, and you're striving to reach a 3.0 cumulative GPA for your college career. A 3.5 senior-year GPA won't be good enough—you'll need a 3.6 or better.

previous years insulated her from a more precipitous drop. But a freshman, just starting out, hasn't built any consistency. So a C combined with three B's results in a 2.75 GPA, whereas straight B's would have netted a 3.0 GPA.

While no student aspires to straight Cs, there are worse grades, namely D and F. Nothing devastates a GPA like an F, since it's figured into the cumulative index like a zero. At many schools, students have the option of retaking a failed course—but there's frequently a catch. Policies vary, but they often allow students to either count the new grade instead of the F, or average the F with the new grade. In either case, the F usually stays on the transcript, and you'll always have to make up the credits to graduate.

It seems freshmen are more likely to get F's than upperclassmen, because experienced students are more mindful of a failing grade's impact. Sean Galusha remembers partying a lot his freshman year at the Community College of Southern Nevada, and getting a couple of F's. "I wasn't taking it seriously," he recalls. He took two years off to work, and—confronted with the possibility of working low-income jobs the rest of his life—changed his ways. He earned acceptance into the University of Nevada–Las Vegas, where he's a member of the class of 2005 and earning better grades. How did he turn it around? "I just grew up."

Whether it's an A student who receives a C, or a B student who receives an F, Adam Abelkop (Wake Forest University, Class of 2007) suggests quickly learning from your blunder, because it's not coming off your transcript. "Everyone has some bad grading experience at one point or another in his or her college career. . . . You're not the only one," says Adam. "Accept the grade and move on. Figure out what went wrong, and work to prevent that from happening again."

When considering what went wrong, Adam has a few ideas: "If you chose a tough professor, be more informed before you select classes next time. If you failed because you didn't study, then study for the next test. If you made warrantless claims in your argumentative paper, find out how to warrant your arguments in the next paper."

If you feel you were graded unfairly, Lauren Hardgrove of Ohio University recommends appealing. "You can always petition to a particular teacher for a better grade, or at least for a chance to make it up," she says.

But such appeals aren't likely to be successful. The process may not necessarily be antagonistic, but face it: You're trying to tell an esteemed faculty member that she made a mistake. She'll likely listen to you carefully and politely, then offer a firm rebuttal. The good news: If she honestly made a mistake, she'll likely correct it. The not-so-good news: If you deserved the grade you received, especially if it's a low one, you may receive a painstaking analysis of your shortcomings.

Whether you do well or not so well your first semester at school, it's a good time to assess what went right and what didn't. Since many students continue with the academic approach that got them to college in the first place, first-semester grades indicate whether that strategy is viable for the future.

> *"[Professors] are much more willing to help than you might think. If you are in a class of 300 people, you might think that they won't have time to speak with you, but if you bomb a midterm and think that all hope is lost, go talk to him or her and let them know that you care about your grades and will do anything to do better in the class."*
>
> —Tanner Sykes, Texas Tech University, Class of 2005

Rosanne Boyle did very well in her studies her first semester at Fairfield University, easing the way for a transfer to Providence College, which was much closer to her Massachusetts home. She was thrilled to be at Providence, and plunged into campus life there, including involvement in the Board of Programmers, a group she would lead in her senior year. "At that point in time I figured I could just continue with what I was doing and end up graduating with a great GPA and be proud of the work I did," she says. "I didn't spend as much time studying as I should've and I ended up disappointing myself, grade-wise. So the next semester I paid more attention to my schoolwork and got better grades. I've done well ever since."

15

Choosing a Major

"The major that you want at 17 or 18 isn't necessarily the major that still interests you at 21 or 22."

—Patrice Williams, Temple University, Class of 2005

"What's your major?" might be the most commonly asked question on college campuses—it's a way of summarizing, in as little as one word, what you're all about. An answer of "philosophy" might evoke one kind of response, while "biology" elicits quite another. Respond with "I don't know yet," and you might as well prepare to answer a few more questions.

This chapter will explore the critical but sometimes laborious process of selecting a major—a focused program of study that may or may not play a significant role in where you work after graduation.

When should I pick my major?

"Before the beginning of junior year."
"ASAP."
"By the end of freshman year."
"Whenever you feel most comfortable."

Those are some of the responses students offered to this question. It reflects the gulf that separates what some wish they did, what some actually did, and what their colleges recommend that they do.

Except for a few untraditional colleges or programs where it's not required, just about every student must formally declare a major, typically by the end of sophomore year or the start of junior year. Since it's a choice fraught with consequences, students who don't know what they want to major in can get stressed out by the process. Indeed, few things can produce as much anxiety for a college student as being unsure of what to major in. (Midterms and finals come close, though.) Yet students can take comfort in the fact that most freshmen aren't sure of their major when they arrive on campus.

One reason for the conflicting guidance about the best time to choose a major is that no single piece of advice takes into account the differences between individual students. All factors being equal, it's obviously better if you know earlier than later—so try to decide early, some recommend. On the other hand, there's no sense rushing into a decision that you might regret—so take your time picking a major, others advise.

About the only certainty is that a decision must be made, and as freshman year slips into sophomore year, the clock begins ticking more audibly. It's true that you shouldn't rush your choice, but you do need to make a decision. Among the many consequences of being undecided are

- ✓ Having to tell people you're still undecided when they ask about your major. That gets old very quickly.
- ✓ Not knowing what classes to schedule because you don't have a major sequence of classes to follow.
- ✓ Waiting too long to decide might make it too hard to fit in all the classes in four years, meaning more time on campus and more tuition to pay.

Selena Moshell (Rollins College, Class of 2005) suggests holding off on choosing a major until at least end of the freshman year—after you've had the chance to explore a diverse range of your college's class offerings. "I can't tell you how many of my friends have gone through four years in one major, and then take one class in another major and then regret four years in a major they thought they were set on," she says.

How do I go about picking a major?

If you really have no clue what you might want to do, that's normal. Meet with an adviser and explain your situation. Your adviser can help you get started by exploring your interests and choosing some classes that could lead to a major. Without such a plan, it's more likely that you'll need additional time to graduate when you finally do decide.

When she was unsure of what to major in, Grace Choe (University of Southern California, Class of 2005) visited a USC career counselor. "There was a shelf with many different handouts describing professions, like nursing, teaching, optometry, writing . . . and the classes you'd need for those professions," explains Grace. She took them home and reviewed them, rejecting those that had math or science requirements. She narrowed her focus to English and journalism, eventually opting for the latter. From there, she settled on a major in public relations. "Now I feel so lucky that I found a major that is so perfectly suited for me."

In most cases, a major won't just present itself; you will find one through a process of self-exploration. You can try some introductory classes in different subject areas, for example—ideally while fulfilling core requirements at the same time. Or you can evaluate careers you might want to explore and see what classes would be needed for such jobs. Either way, you need to ask questions that can help launch you along the right path.

If you're using classes to guide your thinking, you might ask: Do I like this class? Why or why not? What kind of class might I like more instead? How much would I enjoy advanced study in this field? Would I like to specialize in this field? What kind of career would this program of study lead to? What is the job market anticipated to be like when I am ready to start searching for employment in this career area? These questions can help you distinguish between classes that are merely interesting and those that could actually lead to long-term employment. Lisa Hall (University of Louisville, Class of 2004) took this approach: "I just took a lot of electives the first two years, so I could explore a little and figure out what I liked," she explains. "I ended up with marketing."

If you have a career in mind, but not necessarily a program of study, ask yourself what you'd have to do to get there: Could I see myself working in this field as a career? What coursework would I need to declare a major that would lead to this job? Does the coursework appeal to me? These questions can help weed out career choices that are not practical. For example, a career in medicine appeals to lots of high-achieving high-school students. But the massive academic demands, not to mention internships and residency requirements, steer many into other fields once they get to college.

"Students ought to declare a major when they are comfortable saying 'I could do something like this when I graduate,'" says Julia Bauler (Gonzaga University, Class of 2005). Julia switched majors three times before declaring a political science major, and she's glad she didn't settle for something she wasn't energized for.

Julia says her decision to major in political science is the biggest and best choice she's made in college. She's been part of an exchange program that allowed her to spend a semester in Washington, D.C. "The opportunities and experiences I have had because of these decisions are unbelievable," she says. "I have refined and developed my passions in life. If I had chosen another major or field of study, I don't believe I would be as happy or as excited about my future."

Sit In On a Class

Ginger Ruskamp (Creighton University, Class of 2005) has the following suggestions: For those who want to sample many different courses, consider asking a professor if you can sit in on a class a few times. It won't always be possible, but it's a good way of getting a feel for a discipline. And for those who are interested in certain careers but don't really know enough about them, try to find someone to "shadow" for a day, Ginger recommends. Your college's career office may be able to put you in touch with some candidates.

All the Wrong Reasons

Many students who declare their major in response to family pressures end up unhappy, says Marc Wais, the vice president for student affairs at New York University. They might feel obligated to pursue pre-law or a science to follow in a parent's footsteps, for example, or they might choose a business major because they sense an expectation that they need to land a high-paying job upon graduation. But without a strong interest in the subject area they've chosen, they may struggle to get excited about their education. Says Julia Bauler of Gonzaga University: "Ten years down the road a student will only be happy with a career they chose, not in one that they feel pushed into for any number of reasons."

How do I know if a major is right for me?

The way students describe it, finding the right major is a lot like falling in love—it's not the easiest thing in the world to describe, but you know for sure when you've found it.

Maybe you won't see fireworks when your fine-arts professor describes Rembrandt's *chiaroscuro* technique. And perhaps your heart won't race when you dissect a fetal pig in biology class. But you should feel a spark—a sense of excitement—about at least one subject area.

Jarita Lindsey, a social work major at St. Louis University, says a field of study may be right for you if you look forward to attending class, or if you find yourself doing additional research into the subject on your own time.

An "eagerness" to learn more about a field of study indicates you're hot on the trail of a major, says Patrick Cook (Georgia Institute of Technology, Class of 2007). He opted for mechanical engineering as his pre-medicine major at Georgia Tech after thoroughly enjoying—and acing—a physics class that covered mechanical engineering concepts.

> *"It won't take long for you to understand whether or not you belong. Do you feel engaged in the class? Are you generally interested in topics of discussion? Are you excited to learn more in a class that might some day help you in the field? These are questions that will help you know if you are in the right place."*
>
> —Tanner Sykes, Texas Tech University, Class of 2005

Conversely, there are times when a field of study doesn't fit right. Lindy Pennington (University of Nevada–Las Vegas, Class of 2005) is a civil engineering major. He had started off as a biochemistry major, but soon discovered it was wrong for him. "I realized I didn't want that when I was stuck in the lab for hours . . . bored," he says.

If you're bored by it, don't do well in the classes, or are not interested in the idea of advanced study in the field, it may be best to find something else.

But what if you realize this after you've chosen a major? Read on.

What do I do if I want to switch my major?

Students who change majors are about as common as students who like late nights and pizza. It's such a routine part of the process that it might be more unusual if one doesn't consider changing majors.

"First there was pre-med—then psychology and education," says Erica Lemansky (Brandeis University, Class of 2005). "Somewhere along the line I thought about neareastern Judaic studies, and I've taken classes in sociology, philosophy, American studies, and chemistry, just to name a few." She opted for a psychology major with a minor in education studies, and isn't bothered by the tortuous road she traveled to arrive at her final choice. "That's what college is for—exploring options, taking in all that you can, and deciding what is right for you."

Jamie Simchik (Colgate University, Class of 2007) was equally intrigued by his school's diverse course offerings. "I entered Colgate with the intention of being an astrophysics major," he says. "That did not happen. . . . I took Intro to Econ and realized that I enjoyed Econ more."

For those who show up on campus determined to major in a field, the decision to drop a major can be more difficult than finding a field to study.

Kevin McPherson (University of Texas at Austin, Class of 2007) first majored in electrical engineering. He did well, grade-wise, his first semester, but that wasn't enough to keep him happy. "I just couldn't stand what I was learning," he recalls. Two weeks into the second semester, he decided he was in the wrong field. "It wasn't an easy decision. I thought I would be labeled a quitter, but I couldn't make my decision based on that. I did a lot of praying about it, and I felt that engineering was not where I was supposed to be—it wasn't where my heart and passion was. So I dropped it. I changed to business and possibly music. That's what I enjoy doing and that's where I feel I should be."

University of Pittsburgh student Danielle Kittredge dropped her engineering major after a year. "I knew right away it was something I didn't want to do anymore," says Danielle (Class of 2006). She promptly switched to urban planning. She says that if she kept going with engineering, she might have felt obliged to continue because of the great investment in time and money. It made her choice easier when she got to know a Pitt junior who was an engineering major, and saw the future for herself: "I realized that he was unhappy with his decision, and if I stayed, I would have been unhappy."

Jamie Veasey recalls arriving at the University of Evansville prepared to embark on her lifelong goal of being a veterinarian. "After two years of college, I changed my mind," says Jamie (Class of 2005). She decided she wanted to pursue psychology instead. She credits a helpful Evansville psychology professor with helping her change paths at the midpoint of her college career. Looking back, she has no regrets about switching. "It can be really stressful, but it is worth it."

A Matter of Timing

One of the biggest factors to consider when changing majors is how you'll complete your studies in your new field. While it's true that a student shouldn't be miserable in her chosen field of study, there comes a point—sometime after the beginning of junior year and obviously before the end of senior year—when it's less practical to switch.

Some classes needed for a major are only offered once a year. If you switch into the new program during the "off" semester, you could lose vital time.

It's always possible to switch majors, but it may take another year of college—or more, if you decide to switch at an especially late point. That's not a problem for students with the time and financial resources to do so. But for the less affluent, the real decision is whether they can afford to take on more debt after their fourth year of college, instead of taking a job to pay down college loans.

Of course, just because you consider switching majors, it doesn't mean you have to do it. Consider it a flirtation.

That's what happened with Patrice Williams (Temple University, Class of 2005). She chose an English major because she loves literature and writing. But in her junior year, she checked out education and social work. "My interests changed, so I figured I might change my major as well," says Patrice. The prospect of changing majors at that point in college scared her, but she still seriously considered switching, even if it meant taking longer to graduate. In the end, however, she chose to stay with English.

Although it's common to switch majors, it's still a big decision—one that's best made in consultation with advisers.

Alan Kastler (Southwest Missouri State University, Class of 2005) switched majors twice; each time, he talked with his adviser before signing the paperwork. "We would look at whether the change would set me back in graduation, see what new requirements I had, and made sure that the decision I was making was the right one," he says. "One thing to look at when changing majors is how many credits will you lose?"

Alan started off majoring in agricultural business finance/management. After freshman year, he decided he didn't want to go into agriculture, so he switched to general business/finance. After sophomore year, he narrowed his focus to administrative management. Alan did not lose any academic ground, despite the time it took to arrive at his major; he credits his adviser with helping him stay ahead on his requirements.

Should I double-major?

Double-majoring may be one of the last great values in a college education. Those who pursue this plan end up with a strong background in two subject areas, instead of one.

But does it pay off? It depends on the reasons for choosing such a course. Those who are passionate about two subject areas, and who are double-majoring for their own personal fulfillment, are likely to be happy with their decision. On the other hand, those who expect a significant benefit in the job market may be misguided.

"You should have an interest in both of your majors or else you will work hard on the one you like and slack off on the one you don't," says Alyssa Limberakis (Syracuse University, Class of 2006), who originally started off majoring only in public relations—the field she wants to pursue as a career.

"I chose political science as my other major in order to narrow the huge field of communications," adds Alyssa, a dean's list student. "I actually think I would be bored if I had only one major. . . . It also doesn't hurt to beef up the resume a little bit."

Despite the intensive work she'll face in upper-level classes, Rebekah Lee (Rutgers University, Class of 2007) is excited about her pre-medicine double-major in biology and history. "I love both of these subjects—my history classes are more fun than work—so these classes are very interesting for me."

Students need to declare both majors early enough that they can take their required classes within four years. Doing so, however, can be difficult. The introductory classes for both majors could be scheduled at the same time. Or the two majors might be "housed" in different "schools" within the university—each with distinct policies that may not work in harmony.

Laurie Quaife, for example, graduated from Kansas State University in 2004 with a double-major in criminology and political science. Both degree programs are housed in KSU's College of Arts and Science, meaning core degree requirements were the same for both majors. "All of my general education requirements counted for both [majors]," she says. "For me, my classes for one major counted as some of my electives for the other, and vice versa. If you plan ahead, you can often figure out ways for more than one program to fit together." Choosing a double-major worked out well, she says, because it allowed her to pursue two separate interests of hers. She suggests that students torn between two fields explore the possibility of majoring in both.

Richa Bhala (Amherst College, Class of 2007) gently throws some cold water on the fires of those ready to sign up for two majors. She points out a primary argument against this: that by focusing on two fields of study, little room may be left to receive a well-rounded liberal arts education. As a result, some schools strongly discourage double-majors, while others do not allow them.

On a different level, a dual major may make it difficult for students to spend a semester abroad, because they will have so many requirements to fulfill. Lastly, when it comes to job-seeking, most employers tend to look at your overall experience and whether you're a good "fit." A degree in two fields may not hurt, but it may not boost one's chances, either.

Many students who double-major say it wasn't what they originally intended to do.

Bryant Jones (University of Vermont, Class of 2005) began as a biology major—a course of study demanding enough on its own—with no intention of adding another. But that soon changed. He took a course in comparative democratization and developed a keen interest in political science. Before long, he was majoring in both subject areas.

"I had heard scary things about how hard it was and that you have to take a lot more classes," says Bryant "I had put lots of time into my biology major and did not want that to go to waste. I felt that I could pull it off and achieve two majors. I was determined that if I put in the effort things would pay off, and they have."

Bryant recommends checking with an adviser about double-majoring as soon as you have in inkling about it. He was especially inspired to pursue his dual major because his adviser, Assistant Professor Lisa M. Holmes, majored in the same two fields as a Vermont undergraduate before earning a master's degree and Ph.D. at the University of Georgia.

Advisers can help students figure out exactly what they'll need to do to double-major, and, critically, how much time they'll need to do it.

If you're having trouble seeing an adviser, don't take no for an answer, because this is an area where a delay could be costly. Knock on the door of the dean or the chancellor, if necessary, so that you can get the advisement you need to make the right decisions for your future.

Does a minor/concentration really matter?

Let's say you run a firm that specializes in environmental studies, and a recent college graduate walks in the door, seeking a job.

You'd likely ask her about her qualifications for the job, her interest in the field, and why she thinks she'd fit in well with the firm.

Would you ask her about her ability to dance? Probably not.

Does that mean Selena Moshell, an environmental studies major, made the wrong choice when she decided to minor in dance at Rollins College? Not at all. The major matters most. Although she says she's passionate about her major, before she goes to graduate school for further study she wants to work in the dance field.

"Even though my major and minor don't exactly go hand in hand, they allow me to fully explore my potential," says Selena. "The dance minor has been perfect for me to keep my technique up, to strengthen my performance skills, and to work with amazing guest choreographers."

It also shows that she's multidimensional.

A minor usually entails taking about five or six classes in a given field, about half of what's needed to major in a subject area. Rarely is a minor a factor in a student's success in college, or in landing a job. But—like a minor character in a movie—it can play a big part in the outcome of things.

Jennifer George (Wake Forest University, Class of 2004) majored in computer science with a minor in journalism. But a funny thing happened along the way: "It may turn out that the subject you choose as a minor is something that you like a lot more than your major," she says. Jennifer is now exploring graduate school options in journalism.

> *"A minor can strengthen a major to which you're already dedicated, or a minor can be an outlet for another potential career you'd like to foster, but not as a major."*
>
> —Selena Moshell, Rollins College, Class of 2005

For some students, like Selena Moshell, a minor provides a chance to show a completely different side of themselves—one not normally associated with their intended career path. A minor can be something students select based almost solely on the personal fulfillment it provides. That's not to say it's not important—it's just that prospective employers will probably view it as little more than a strength that may not necessarily be related to the position at hand.

Meredith Schweitzer (Vanderbilt University, Class of 2006), for example, chose to minor in music because it's a field she loves. And with a dual major in elementary education and English, she'll already have plenty of academic credentials when she seeks employment. "I've been taking various music classes throughout college—classes such as 'Beethoven and the Beatles'—and they have almost always been my favorite classes each semester," says Meredith, who's also secretary of the Vanderbilt University Concert Choir. "It's very helpful to find an area that really interests you, or classes that you truly look forward to going to."

Similarly, Bryant Jones says he always wanted to learn more about Chinese culture, history, and language, so he chose to minor in Asian studies. "I don't see that a major in Asian studies will take me very far professionally, but a minor allows me to pursue my passion to learn about the Middle Kingdom of China and learn its language."

For other students, a minor serves as a more natural extension of the major choice; it's a specialty within a specialty. While a minor doesn't need to be such an extension, it clearly makes sense in some fields.

Patrick Cook, whose pre-medicine major at Georgia Tech is mechanical engineering, chose to minor in biomedical engineering. "This will help prepare me for the MCAT examination, which will get me into a better medical school," he says.

Samantha Del Priore (Seton Hall University, Class of 2006), a communications major, chose to minor in Spanish. Although some have suggested to her that a minor's only role is to show that you have an outside interest, she sees it differently. "A lot of jobs prefer bilingual employees, so I am trying really hard to learn Spanish," says Samantha.

A Few Good Minors

It's possible to minor in almost anything at college, and rarely is there a bad choice. Here are just a few possibilities:

- ✓ **Foreign language:** Great for those working in metropolitan areas or those who foresee interacting with non-English-speaking clients or colleagues.
- ✓ **Journalism:** Demonstrates that you can write clearly, and without lots of useless, redundant, unnecessary, and really needless clutter.
- ✓ **Biology:** Shows that you have an understanding of the fundamentals of scientific inquiry.
- ✓ **Political science:** Establishes that you know how the world of government and politics works.
- ✓ **Fine arts:** Shows that you have an appreciation of art and culture.

16

Relationships

> ***Most likely, you will have regrets. I know I do. But learn from your mistakes.***
>
> —Codie Thurston, University of Alaska Anchorage, Class of 2006

Ginger Ruskamp (Creighton University, Class of 2005) started college with a long-distance boyfriend. Three years later, at the beginning of her senior year, she points out that they've stayed together because each leads a strong, separate life, where friends and activities play big roles. "This helped us each develop friendships outside of our relationship and has ultimately made our relationship stronger," says Ginger.

Drew Koch (University of South Dakota, Class of 2007) saw a romance start to get serious early in his college career and decided he didn't want to go that route. He broke it off. "I feel the best plan for myself is to casually date girls from time to time and let things take care of themselves later in life," says Drew.

There are countless stories in between Drew's and Ginger's experiences, with a few on the following pages. Wherever your "relationship status" falls on the spectrum—and it will likely be at different points through the years—it will affect your college experience, for better or worse. This chapter explores some of the issues that will surface as students chart their own relationship course.

Should I date someone exclusively?

When students address this question, they sound as if they're talking about choosing a major. Specifically, they mention keeping their options open, from playing the field to making a commitment. Just as some students take their time choosing a major, others feel no need to commit to a boyfriend or girlfriend. Just as some stick with the major they declared during freshman year, some stay with a steady partner during college. Another parallel: Many students, after they've chosen a major, drop it for another—either because they discover the first choice is not what it's cracked up to be, or because something better comes along.

The constant is that no matter what students do, they're motivated by what they believe to be best for them.

"I don't think you should decide anything about relationships until you actually meet a person," says Kim Powers (Ithaca College, Class of 2005). Kim's perspective changed after she arrived at the college, located in Central New York. She began school fresh off a break-up, intending to live commitment-free and to enjoy single life. That lasted less than three weeks, at which time she met and became involved with a junior transfer student. They shared lots of common ground, and a serious relationship blossomed. Even though that wasn't her original plan, it has worked for her. "You don't have to date around, but you don't have to date exclusively," she says. "Each person is different."

Erin Malony (University of Kentucky, Class of 2007) found herself in almost identical circumstances. At the beginning of her sophomore year, she says she does not regret being in a year-long relationship. "But I still keep an open mind," Erin says. "That is the single most important thing about dating in college. Never close your mind and assume you'll be with that person forever." She says students who assume their first passionate relationship will automatically go the distance are making a big mistake: "People tend to assume that this one person is 'it'—and it probably isn't. Date who you want, however you want—but keep looking around, especially in the first year or two of college."

Several students endorsed the concept of a rough split in the college years when it comes to their approach to relationships. They see the first half of college as a time of discovering yourself—not necessarily how your life fits in with someone else's. A too-serious relationship in the first or second year of college has the potential to complicate or limit that period of self-discovery, they say. Later on, perhaps in junior or senior year, after seeing what's out there, students will have a much better idea of what they're getting into—and what they're missing—with relationships. That's not to say that junior and senior year need to be devoted to "finding someone," of course—just that students are in a better position then to make an informed decision about having a serious boyfriend or girlfriend.

> *"I jumped into an exclusive relationship my freshman year . . . and I regret being so young and so committed. There were lots of things I missed out on that I'll never be able to experience."*
>
> —Becca Hatton, West Virginia University, Class of 2005

Becca Hatton (West Virginia University, Class of 2005) estimates that three-quarters of the women in her freshman-year dorm had formal romances with boyfriends back at home. The end results were painful for too many of them, at a time when they should have been practically carefree. "They either went home every weekend—what's the point of paying lots of money for something you never truly experience?—or they cheated on their boyfriends, which lead to guilt and break-ups and unnecessary tears."

Drew Koch headed off such an ugly situation by breaking off a relationship that began to turn more serious than he wanted it to be. "I'm too young to get into a serious relationship," he says, near the beginning of his sophomore year. "I have all of these goals and dreams, and I feel that a serious relationship will only prevent me from reaching those goals and living those dreams."

Sabryna Phillips (Loyola Marymount University, Class of 2006) agrees that college students should not rush into relationships. It's the perfect place to meet people, she says, and those who "settle down" too early are denying themselves that great opportunity. "I have met so many amazing guys throughout my college career, and while I am dating someone exclusively at the moment, he was not the first guy to walk through the door. I figure you have the rest of your life to settle down," she says.

She realizes, though, that like any guidance offered on any subject, students have to be smart in its application. She adds: "If you think you have found a good match, don't let it slip away merely because you are in college."

Should I try to maintain a long-distance romance?

Sheldon Browning (Utah State University, Class of 2005) has seen both sides of this issue. He can't blame students for wanting to persevere with long-distance relationships while in college. On the other hand, he can see why being unattached is the better choice for others. He sees it as something that can only be evaluated on a case-by-case basis—no absolute rules apply.

"If you think the person is worth it, then definitely yes—even if it seems like it may 'hurt' your college experience, college is not the most important thing in life," he says. "I have been in a relationship that I knew had the potential of making life at college more of a challenge while she was away, but I felt so strongly that she was worth it. And guess what—she ended up breaking my heart. But that doesn't necessarily mean that it was a bad decision."

Students interviewed about this issue shared some consistencies: They are not opposed to long-distance relationships or romance. But they feel that so many students in those relationships appear to miss out on something, whether it's quality time with their campus friends, or that invigorating collegiate sense of independence and freedom. And they observe that much more often than not, the relationships fail.

The consensus is that if you have a long-distance relationship that's making you happier, friendlier, funnier, and a better person, then stick with it. If it's making you leave school with reluctance every weekend, limit your socializing on campus, and worry about your boyfriend or girlfriend's new study partner, then by all means, bail out and get on with your life.

Signals to Drop a Long-Distance Relationship

- ✓ You fight frequently. Having a boyfriend or girlfriend at college should mean many more good times than bad ones.
- ✓ Either partner is jealous of the other's enjoyment of college life, whether it's late nights or plutonic relationships with members of the opposite sex. Who needs that nonsense?
- ✓ You sometimes use an alias screen name so that your boyfriend/girlfriend can't see you or instant message you online.
- ✓ You or your boyfriend/girlfriend are losing sincere enthusiasm in the relationship; it's getting to be a hassle to call/visit/e-mail.
- ✓ You feel like you can't fully enjoy your college experience.

Valerie Rozycki and her friends at Stanford University haven't had much luck when it comes to long-distance relationships. "I tried . . . and it didn't last very long," says Valerie (Class of 2005). "My friends have tried . . . and those didn't last either. One friend started dating a guy from home later in freshman year and the relationship lasted until late in her senior year, but even that fell apart eventually."

Valerie says she's learned that even though long-distance relationships can work, they may not be the healthiest thing for one's independent growth—a critical aspect of college. "Learning about other people and other types of relationships is extremely important for the individual—and even ultimately important for the couple, if they are really meant to be," she says.

"So many freshmen miss out on meeting new people because they are always visiting their boyfriends or girlfriends, and they really regret it later," says Kristina Ihlenfeldt (Clemson University, Class of 2003). Her suggestion: "If you choose to keep it, don't waste all your weekends visiting each other, and make sure you leave plenty of time for making friends and enjoying your first year at college."

Speaking of time invested in long-distance relationships, the Internet and free late-night cellphone talk-time have made it easier than ever to devote hours every day to faraway paramours. Boyfriends and girlfriends can exchange instant messages all day, or talk on their cellphones for hours at a time late at night and not incur any charges. Rather than being conveniences, these modern marvels have upped the stakes in long-distance relationships. Students aren't just leaving campus on the weekends to visit their sweethearts—they're spending lots of time communicating with them by instant message, e-mail, or the cellphone.

The investment of time should compel students to ask themselves: Is this relationship the best thing for me?

Melinda Stiles found that it's not. She tried to maintain a year-long high-school relationship when she first arrived at the University of Minnesota, Twin Cities, but it didn't last. "When I got to college, I realized that it was such a different experience from high school and that there were so many more people out there that I had to take a chance and try new things," says Melinda (Class of 2007). "Being with that person was a tie to my past, and almost felt like an obligation. I felt that that relationship would have prevented me from growing and changing into a new person with all of the new experiences I would have."

University of Connecticut student Jessica Bal also continued a high-school romance into her first three semesters at UConn. While it didn't work out in the long run, she's not as regretful as some of her peers. She doesn't feel she lost out on anything because the relationship was honest and open. "It's all about communication," she says, while offering this advice to new college students: "Don't be close-minded about the opportunities to meet new people around you, but also appreciate a solid relationship while you have it."

Sean Carroll (University of Illinois at Urbana–Champaign, Class of 2004) says the best way to decide whether a long-distance relationship is worthwhile is to have an honest conversation—with yourself: "If you are looking in a book for the answer to this question, you have some serious problems," he says, much to the chagrin of this book's publisher. "No one can tell you this but yourself."

What should I consider before hooking up with someone?

"Hooking up" can mean very different things to different people, students point out. To some, it means a brief kiss and nothing more. To others, it involves varying amounts of sexual contact. As most students define it, there is no commitment to the other beyond that moment.

When it comes to hooking up, students say their plainest advice, based on what they've experienced, is to know who you are; know who your partner is; know what you each expect; know that there are risks; and be cautious.

"Each individual has personal beliefs, morals, values, and ideals that define them from the next person," says Codie Thurston (University of Alaska Anchorage, Class of 2006). Her suggestion: Respect others' values and hold true to your own, whatever they are.

Codie, who hails from Lander, Wyoming (population: 6,867), realized she'd have wide latitude to draw her own boundaries when she arrived at UAA. "Now that there was no curfew [and] no parents to meet the 'boyfriend,' it was okay to do what I wanted," she recalls. But she saw that the stakes were higher in college, and she did her best to be careful; for her, the process was one of trial and error. "Most likely, you will have regrets," she points out to new students. "I know I do. But learn from your mistakes." How? "Be assertive and don't settle."

To avoid a situation you'll regret, Kim Powers of Ithaca College suggests asking yourself some questions that can help you set guidelines: How well do you know the other person? Are any factors affecting the judgment of either of you? What are the expectations of both of you? These questions are admittedly difficult to weigh in the heat of the moment, but they're still important to consider in those situations. "In many instances, we don't have time to think about considerations before hooking up with someone," she acknowledges. "It's hard to think about all these things, and with each person, guidelines vary. It's important to know what you want, and to stay strong on those values."

Aside from the values issue, the specter of major health-related problems looms over any sexual relationship. Contracting a disease and plunging into a depression should not be on anyone's mind when having sex. But those things, along with the clear possibility of pregnancy, must be—especially for college students. Those who don't consider these to be real possibilities are fools.

Reading words of caution about sexual situations in the cold light of day—when it may be tough to relate to the circumstances—can prompt students to roll their eyes at the suggestions. They're based on common sense, after all. But students don't always follow common sense. The story of the following student illustrates how even the most seemingly responsible people can get caught in agonizing situations.

The student, cited in several sections of this book but kept anonymous here, explains how a friend of hers, who generally knows her limits, had an experience that no student would ever want to endure. The friend was drunk, which is how a lot of bad stories involving college life start off. Then she ran into an ex-boyfriend.

"She called me the next morning, sounding terrible," the student's friend relates. "Not only did she let herself down, but she complicated her relationship with this guy, put herself at a risk for STDs, lost her virginity while drunk, and had to deal with the horror of a potential unwanted pregnancy."

Clearly affected by her friend's plight, the student admonishes those new to college: "All I can say is learn from her mistake. The goal should be to have no regrets about your sexual history: who, when, under what conditions. . . ."

Having sex when it's not what you planned can lead to much more than despair, depression, or hurt feelings, as serious as those things are. The possible physical consequences of sex—unplanned pregnancies and a host of sexually transmitted diseases, including AIDS—can't be understated.

Students, backed by college health administrators nationwide, urge those who choose to have sex to take precautions against unplanned pregnancies and sexually transmitted diseases. Many colleges provide low-cost or free services, ranging from contraception counseling to STD tests. If yours does not provide these services and you want them, a counselor or resident adviser should be able to offer direction.

Clearly, a romance, however brief, can be a thrilling, powerful part of the college experience. But like it or not, that power can be positive or negative. Those who balance the power with responsibility are likely to have fewer regrets.

How can I tell if I'm wasting my time in a relationship?

How do you know when it's time to get out of a relationship? If we were to sum up the answers that follow, they'd all be a variation on "You just know."

Sabryna Phillips of Loyola Marymount University says it comes down to instinct. For example, if you feel you're putting more into the relationship than your significant other, you're probably wasting your time: "There is bound to be someone else out there for you," she says.

Listen to your heart, advises Drew Koch of the University of South Dakota. That's what he did when he examined the feelings of depression he had in his gut while dating someone. "I couldn't figure out what the cause of it was, but I soon realized the gut feeling was my heart telling me that the relationship I was in was going nowhere," he remembers.

To avoid those "nowhere" relationships, Adam Lucido (Montana State University–Billings, Class of 2006) suggests not getting too contented. Here's his litmus test: Is the relationship meaningful and a top priority for me, or is it just comfortable? "If you choose the latter, the red flags should go up," he says, speaking from his own experiences. "I made this very mistake with a girl. Things were just so routine and comfortable, yet not necessarily satisfying and enjoyable. I didn't love the person; I simply favored the ease and comfort of the situation."

Adam knows he's made a common mistake. He's learned how tough it can be to grow personally if you get too comfortable with any aspect of life when you're barely 19 or 20.

Like Adam, Becky Thilo (Rice University, Class of 2007) also has a test to see how a romance is going: "It's all in how you react when they call," she says. "If caller ID shows that your significant other is calling and your stomach does a little flip or a smile springs across your face, there is no need to worry. However, if there is a lump of dread in your gut and you hesitate in answering the phone, that's a good sign you're in a bad relationship."

Of course, she points out another possibility: If your phone isn't ringing (and you're not racing to place a call either) it's possible the two of you don't really have time for a relationship. Or each other. So it might be time to move on.

"College is a crazy time with lots to do," Becky says. "If prioritizing a relationship is not in your plans, then you are wasting the time of both people."

Time is what it frequently comes down to for students assessing their relationships. If they're sincerely enjoying the moments with their boyfriend or girlfriend, and the romance is not holding them back from enjoying other key aspects of college life, the couple is at least off to a good start. But, as Bradley Baker of the University of Mississippi points out, if you feel pressured to spend every free moment with your sweetheart, it probably means you need to spend time apart.

Is there room on campus for students with "old-fashioned" values?

If one thing is emphasized in college life, it's the importance of being yourself. The many students who say there is plenty of room for those with "old-fashioned" values make their point not because of moral reasons, but because individuality is so highly respected on campus.

"They are welcome with open arms," says Sabryna Phillips of the "old-fashioned" students. "In fact, the people who have strong values tend to be respected a great deal and many times others wish they had stuck to the same standards. College is all about being yourself—and others will accept you for that if you are not self-conscious about your life decisions."

Students who don't lower their standards will be admired as leaders, says Adam Lucido of Montana State University–Billings, because fellow students realize that it's not always easy going against the grain.

Nonetheless, the first weeks of school, when signs of excess are plentiful on most college campuses, can be intimidating to new students.

They need to realize that not everyone is having sex, taking drugs, and getting drunk all the time, says Chris Diem (Texas A & M University, Class of 2005). "If you're strong in your beliefs, you'll be fine," he says, advising students to stick to their ideals.

Jake Carter (Northwestern University, Class of 2006) concurs that there are times when students may feel like nobody else shares their standards. But no matter what kind of college you're attending, he says, "there will be students who share your mindset—the key is to find those people."

Those who do will soon realize that plenty of other students are just like them, students say. Adds another student: "If you are a person with 'old-fashioned' values—relationship-related or otherwise—there is a group of people out there with similar beliefs and values." This student revealed how her roommate, for example, eschews drinking and the party scene in favor of dancing and music-related activities. "She couldn't be happier," the student relates, adding that her roommate met a guy because she got out and got involved, not because she tried to adjust her values. "It's definitely possible."

Chelsea Church (Michigan State University, Class of 2006) says she could be considered a student with "old-fashioned" values. But she says she has not regretted holding true to her beliefs one bit. Chelsea observed what was going on with her peers her freshman year, but simply decided, "That wasn't me." She says she quickly realized that there's more to college life than parties, guys, and alcohol. "There are so many things that universities provide beyond such things," she says, citing everything from student organizations to sports and religious activities. "Be true to yourself or you won't be happy with life."

Should I move in with my boyfriend/girlfriend?

Some arrived at their position on this subject through firsthand experience. "Moving in with my girlfriend was probably the worst mistake of my collegiate career," says Adam Lucido.

Others reached their conclusions by watching their relationships with their friends sour: "Many of my friends have . . . eventually moved in with their significant other—and then they disappear," says Sabryna Phillips.

And many simply can't imagine why anyone would want to sacrifice their limited personal space during a time of life that's supposed to be all about independence.

Coed living is not an option in college-sponsored two-person dorm rooms, but students are free to mix genders in off-campus apartments, where many live during junior and senior years. While students interviewed don't categorically condemn living with a boyfriend or girlfriend, they say the potential drawbacks, for everyone involved, far outweigh the potential benefits.

Adam Lucido says the formalities of living together with his girlfriend—from socializing together to financial matters—made him feel trapped. "[It] killed our relationship," he says. "I felt even more miserable in that I still had to live with this person—talk about being caught between a rock and a hard place." He admits that it might seem logical for couples to move in together, since they spend so much time with each other in the first place. But convenience is only one factor to be considered.

Personal space is perhaps the biggest. Students living with their boyfriend or girlfriend can possibly feel they have no space to themselves, given that the pair probably shares the bathroom, kitchen, and bills—and perhaps the bedroom. The only "escape" is class or work time—unless, of course, those hours are shared, too. That closed-in feeling, if it surfaces, has the potential to breed resentment and fuel a break-up faster than a fling with an old flame.

But even when couples are happy to spend every waking minute together, they're usually doing so at the expense of time with their friends. And anecdotal evidence suggests that "friend neglect" is a frequent byproduct of a college couple's cohabitation. The couple may not notice until months have passed that they've missed critical time with friends.

"I am lucky to see them in passing on the way to class," says Sabryna Phillips, regarding friends who are too wrapped up with their live-in paramours. "I do not think that is any way to spend your college career."

Erin Malony has had similar experiences. "I don't see my friends who live with their significant others nearly as much as I see others," she says. The first thing to go when a couple moves in together, from what she's observed, is quality time with friends of the same gender. In those cases, either the couple neglects the friends, or the friends aren't comfortable hanging out when they know their pal's boyfriend or girlfriend is always very close by.

"While I'm sure this is a compromise that must be reached when you get married . . . you aren't married yet. Living together is a big step that signifies an incredibly deep commitment—which, during college, when you don't even know who *you* are, maybe isn't the best thing."

> *"My opinion isn't even morally or religiously based on this one [issue]. You have the rest of your life to live with your loved one. Live with your friends. You'll regret missing the girl (or boy) time."*
>
> —Chelsea Church, Michigan State University, Class of 2006

17

Money

One of my best collegiate decisions has been to forego the mountain of credit-card offers that I receive daily. While it is tempting at times . . . I'm better off not having that monthly payment.

—Adam Lucido, Montana State University–Billings, Class of 2006

Some students may be in for a surprise when their parents don't send them chunks of money to pay for their pizzas, movie nights, and haircuts at college. That's because Mom and Dad may be suffering from college sticker shock themselves, writing a check for up to $3,000 a month to cover tuition, room and board, and maybe (if you're fortunate) books and supplies. It's likely they've had to make some big sacrifices to send you to college, so it only makes sense that you share the burden. As a result, they frequently draw the line at paying for day-to-day expenses.

For those expenses, students need to either get a part-time job or do without. The other option—credit—is unattractive for reasons that are explored in this chapter. Regardless, frugality, to some degree, often becomes a way of life for students.

This chapter will explore some of the issues that students face when it comes to managing their money and expenses—how much to work a part-time job, how to handle credit and the debt that often follows, and how to keep expenses down. The chapter also explores some rewarding job possibilities and offers suggestions on checking them out.

How much should I work at a part-time job?

Adam Lucido (Montana State University–Billings, Class of 2006) recalls the spring semester of his freshman year, when he had a nice block of empty space on his schedule Tuesday and Thursday afternoons. It made sense, then, to fill up those hours by working at the Italian restaurant near campus where he was employed. He'd be finished in time those days to attend an evening class, English 301—Business Communication. But something happened between serving all that pasta and the start of class. He was exhausted, and frequently skipped the class. Adam still managed to do well in his assignments, so he wasn't overly concerned. But playing hooky caught up to him. "The instructor stated, 'You do good work, but I couldn't overlook six absences,' from which he handed me my final grade on a piece of paper with 'C' on it."

Lesson learned.

In the semesters that followed, Adam says he scheduled his work in such a way that it wouldn't interfere with classes. He resisted the temptation to fill all the open boxes on his schedule grid with work because he saw that some of those boxes needed to stay empty.

Students' semester grades don't just reflect how well they did in class—they show how well they balanced their lives. Few things can motivate students to reassess the relative importance of their jobs like a bad grade, or worse—a string of bad grades that lands them on academic probation.

Making Your Job Work for You

These suggestions have served students well as they've attempted to balance their part-time jobs with their academic commitments:

✓ **Find a flexible employer.** Find a job that's willing to accommodate your unique situation as a student. That means not having to select your classes based on the hours you work. This is where it's best to work for your own college, if you can, says Debbie Mattson of the University of Alaska Anchorage. "They generally tend to be more flexible with your class schedule, especially around finals week."

✓ **Be flexible yourself.** Early in the semester, when things are quieter academically, agree to put in a few more hours on occasion if your employer needs the help. Aside from receiving more money, which will pull you through on a week when you work less, it might earn you the goodwill you need if you're going to make a special request for yourself later in the semester.

✓ **Give yourself a break.** Students are more likely to burn out if they let their jobs consume every free moment. "Have one night off for yourself—preferably a Friday, Saturday, or Sunday—because you need at least one night to enjoy yourself and have a good time," says Russell Schafer (Rice University, Class of 2007).

✓ **Start slowly.** The best way to know your working-hour limit is to start out with a low number of hours—perhaps 8 or 10 a week—and then see how much more you can handle with everything else going on in your life. "Adjust as the year goes on and you have a better feel for how your schedule fits together," says Amelia Hall of the University of Rochester.

Brittany Duke, who's paying her own way through school, admits that it's tempting to think you can always put in more hours on the job. But there's a limit, at which point schoolwork is among the first thing to suffer. She suggests working as much as possible during the summer, when school is usually not a factor in the equation, and trying to stretch that money through a good portion of the school year. Once classes have resumed, she says, plan your schedule so that you work as little as you need to.

Amelia Hall (University of Rochester, Class of 2007) tries to limit herself to 10 hours a week—15 tops—at her campus job. The occasions where she clocked closer to 20 took their toll on her academics and social life, says Amelia, a biology major. "I didn't have as much time to focus on homework as I wanted to, nor did I have much time to sleep, or eat."

Some students, depending on their class schedules, the intensity of their classes, and their study habits, can work more hours. But everyone still has a limit.

Seth Chambers (University of Kentucky, Class of 2004) found out his limit the hard way. During his sophomore year, he worked at an icehouse for around 35 hours a week; it turned out to be more than he could handle. "The job controlled all of my study time and my grades made a huge drop," says Seth, also a bio major. "I realized that the time spent at a job and the money you may earn is not worth the loss of your college education." The following year, he got a job at a bike shop near campus, working about 20 hours a week. It worked out well, giving him the right combination of spending money and time to tend to his academics.

One thing college students should expect from their part-time jobs is a measure of flexibility. No matter how good a student you are, there will be occasions when you might need time off from work—to study or to fulfill some other important obligation. If the job is inflexible, either prepare to work around it, by finishing papers or studying for tests well in advance, or find another job.

Most small businesses can be flexible, but they have their limits. You might be expected to work a Saturday or Sunday each weekend, and get a replacement if you plan to go away. And if you have a conflict, it's best to let your boss know about it beforehand instead of calling in "sick" at the last minute.

The 20-Hour Rule

For those who work campus jobs, many schools have a "20-hour rule," in which students employed by the college cannot work more than that many hours in a given week. But that only applies to on-campus jobs–not if you work at the pizza shop down the street. In those cases, don't expect the boss to automatically give you off Saturday afternoon because you worked 5 to 10 p.m. Tuesday through Friday. She's probably not counting your hours unless you're about to be paid overtime. And even on campus, enforcement of the "20-hour rule" may be lax, since state labor laws generally allow college-age (18 and older) students to work as much as they want because they are adults.

So while your employer may not keep a close watch on the number of hours you work, you should. "Generally, working more than 20 hours is going to really stretch you thin," says Debbie Mattson (University of Alaska Anchorage, Class of 2007), a criminal justice major. During her freshman year, she held down two part-time jobs and kept her hours under that threshold. It worked for her.

Should I accept that great-sounding credit-card offer?

It's a sure thing—a slam dunk. Whether or not you already have a credit card, you will be bombarded with offers to sign up for one shortly after you start freshman year. Fliers will be posted on campus bulletin boards. Advertisements will abound in school publications and magazines you read. And your mailbox will be flooded with offers that seem too good to pass up.

During his freshman year, Ben Starsky (Arizona State University, Class of 2007) signed up for a credit card—and lived to tell about it!

That's because he regularly checked his balance on the card's Web site, so his bills never got out of hand. He only charged what he was certain he could pay off every month. And he never carried a balance, never paid interest, and built his credit rating over the course of the year. It ended up working out well for him.

But Ben's buddy across the hall wasn't so prudent. He liked his first credit card so much that he signed on for another; each received plenty of use. In little time at all, his debt approached $3,000 and his credit maxed out. He ended up not returning to school for the next year.

"The reason credit-card companies give applications to college students is because they know they will make money on them," says Ben. The companies want college students so badly for several reasons. For one thing, many students regularly run up large bills from carefree expenses, a habit that can be tough to break. When a credit-card company signs up a college student during those carefree spending years of roughly 18 to 30, it stands to make buckets of money during that span, and beyond. (That's why your grandmother's mailbox isn't overflowing with the same volume of offers.)

The credit-card companies already make a profit off your purchases—receiving a kickback from vendors of 2.5 to 4.5 percent of the purchase price. But the companies really make money when students *don't* pay their bills in full. Late fees and interest payments can easily add up to hundreds of dollars a year.

Here's how: A student who carries a $500 balance for a full year will pay roughly $100 in interest alone for the year, when using a credit card that charges an annual percentage rate of 20 percent. If that student is late twice with a monthly payment, that can result in another $60 in charges. Exceeding the credit limit can result in being gouged another $25. That means, roughly, that it's costing you about $135 for every $100 you charged.

The costs get far uglier—and seemingly impossible to pay back—when the carried-over balance rises, as it does for so many students. Just do the math: A $3,000 balance for a year, at the same 20 percent annual rate, can mean $600 in interest before you start paying down your outstanding debt.

How to Spend What You Don't Have

Students who want a credit card, but not the debt, employ many strategies, but they all involve charging only what you can afford:

- ✓ **Pay your bill in full every month.** If you find you can't pay your balance for two straight months, cancel your card. Despite the short-term sting, it's the only way to guarantee your debt does not continue to grow. Although she uses her credit card for many different things, Becky Thilo (Rice University, Class of 2007) always makes sure she's within her means: "I have paid off my credit-card bill every month to avoid paying interest and have never come across any financial problems," says Becky.
- ✓ **Carefully study the terms of your offer.** If you're not sure of something, ask for guidance from someone you can trust, like your parents. For starters, though, check out the annual interest rate, suggests Ritesh Mital (Penn State University, Class of 2007). Also find out if there are any monthly fees, the "grace period" for paying your bills, and late fees if you fail to pay your bill on time. Lastly: "Make sure to find out your credit limit—and don't exceed that."
- ✓ **At all costs, avoid the thinking that you'll pay any credit-card debt when you get out of college and start working full time.** While some students may not have a choice, keep in mind that you'll face lots of other expenses after you graduate—rent, student-loan payments, and car payments, to name three big ones. Your first job out of college will likely not pay a high salary. If you have to spend 35 percent of your limited disposable income paying down your college indulgences on

top of everything else, there will be precious little to spend on yourself. "Many graduated students I've talked to regret very much that they are still paying for fun trips taken in college with using a 'great-sounding' credit card," says Ryan Berney (University of Nebraska-Lincoln, Class of 2007). Adds Bradley Baker of the University of Mississippi: "The last thing you want to do is pay back on something you have done in the past."

✓ **Use a debit card that takes money out of your bank account, instead of a credit card.** "I swipe and the money is immediately gone," says Erin Malony (University of Kentucky, Class of 2007). "Plus, I can never overdraw it, as it's set up to pull from my savings account if my checking is for some reason emptied. This way, I'm never spending money I don't have—and that's probably the best way to go."

✓ **Turn down any "special offer" that promises a premium for signing up.** "No free gift or cute outfit or whatever is worth having bad credit, especially when you are just starting out," says Becca Hatton (West Virginia University, Class of 2005). She made the mistake of signing up for a card in order to help someone's charitable campaign. All she got was a headache from some charges she never made. If you're approached with a similar offer, propose instead to make a cash donation to your friend's cause.

✓ **If you really think you may not be able to control your use of the credit card somewhere, leave it home.** For example, Becca Hatton warns against taking your credit card to a bar: "Most places have at least a 10-buck minimum and then you just end up buying drinks for your 'best friends' that you just met."

If either of the above scenarios seems unpleasant, remember that paying off debt involves not just the pain of writing big checks for purchases made months (or years) ago, but also strictly scaling back your current spending habits so that the debt goes down, instead of merely staying at the same level.

Consider: If charging $350 a month got you into debt, it means you couldn't really afford to spend that much. Let's say you can only really afford $250 a month. You'll probably have to work out a plan whereby you now only charge $150 a month, and use the other $100 to pay down your debt. That will be a painful shift from the spending habits you've grown accustomed to, but that's all you can afford. Remember that the less money you put toward paying off the debt, the longer it will take to pay it off, and the more interest you'll have to pay.

Those situations—and the well-founded fears of them—prompted many students to issue stern warnings to new students about credit-card offers. They acknowledge that credit cards serve a purpose and can be useful in crises. But they also know the high potential for misuse that exists among cash-strapped college students.

Becca Hatton agrees that it's good to have a credit card for bona fide emergencies. But: "Unfortunately buying that new outfit at the Gap or buying a round of drinks for everyone at the bar shouldn't constitute as an emergency."

Becca recalls her parents helping her settle her credit-card debt to avoid high interest payments—and then promptly repaying them through the money she earned at an internship. Among other expenses, she had used her card to finance a trip to New Orleans. Airfare alone was expensive, but she also realized that "a credit card and Bourbon Street do not mix."

A low limit was the only thing that kept Becca from racking up a debt of several thousand dollars, she says, providing the foundation of her guidance for students: "Don't get one with too high a [credit] limit or before you know it you'll be a college grad with $3,000 in debt and no job to pay it off," she says. "That's when the credit places start sending the repo man."

Not wanting to take any chances with credit-card debt, Adam Lucido has avoided the cards completely. Adam instead uses a bank debit card, which takes the money directly out his bank account each time he uses it.

I owe much more money than I can pay back—what should I do?

"Hello, Mom and Dad?"

Calling your parents is one solution if you're over your head in debt. But it's not the only one. For starters, you'll have to face the truth that you need to do something quickly to turn things around. That means cutting back on expenses and doing all that you can to put a dent in your debt.

"Work out a plan," advises David Thompson (Lehigh University, Class of 2006). "If you have a job, set something aside each week. Eat in the dining hall instead of eating pizza. Make sure that whoever you owe knows that you are working to get them the money."

Rice University student Russell Schafer endorses the same general plan, but recommends the additional step of cutting up your credit card. While it may seem drastic, it's the only guaranteed way to ensure that you don't continue to ring up credit charges—charges you're not able to afford.

> *"If you think your parents would be at all willing to listen, tell them your situation and request that they loan you the money instead of a bank. If you do this, however, pay them back. If you don't, they'll likely be unable to help you out in the future if you find yourself in the same situation."*
>
> —Jake Carter, Northwestern University, Class of 2006

As for Mom and Dad? Despite the personal growth gained in solving your problems on your own, you're likely paying a steep price—in the form of interest rates and possibly your credit rating—for this lesson. For that reason, your parents, if they're sympathetic, might be willing to settle your debt if you work out a formal payback plan with them. The benefits? You get the credit-card company off your back, which can be a great feeling; your credit rating will no longer be at risk; and you won't be saddled with huge interest rates. The drawback? You open up your finances to your parents, who've now earned the right to garnish your future earnings until you're back in the black. It can be a humbling experience for students who are doing all they can to declare their independence. But part of being independent is being willing to call for help when you're in the deep end of the pool and can't swim.

Other options:

- ✓ Call your credit-card company and let them know your situation. Don't expect a highly sympathetic ear, but it's better than ignoring those "overdue" notices. The company might set up a payment plan, lower your credit limit, or hold off on assessing a late fee—small steps that will make it easier to get caught up.
- ✓ If you have no choice but to carry a high balance from month to month, ask your credit-card company for a reduced interest rate—or transfer your balance to another card that offers a low introductory rate for at least the first six months or longer. Often, your card issuer will agree to match the interest-rate reduction rather than lose your business completely. Remember the comments above about how badly these companies want your business? Play that to your advantage.
- ✓ Explore counseling resources on campus or contact nonprofit agencies that might be able to help you manage your debt. As always, your resident adviser is a good place to start. If she's not helpful, however, see the director of your residence hall or even a faculty adviser. They may not be able to provide direct help, but they should be able to point you in the right direction.
- ✓ Put in a few extra hours a week on your job and sock that money away for your debt. That small extra effort can make a big difference. Don't overwork yourself, though—your grades will suffer, and it's not worth it.

However you approach your financial crisis, don't panic, suggests Sabryna Phillips (Loyola Marymount University, Class of 2006). "Take a deep breath and take it one day at a time," she says.

How can I get by with a very limited cash flow?

We covered food about 13 chapters ago, didn't we? But we return to it here because students repeatedly cite food costs as a big part of overspending—and a key way to cut down their expenses. Food costs can insidiously absorb a huge portion of students' spending money, whether it's $1 a day for a soda, $4 for an occasional latte, $5 for a fast-food meal every few days, or $20 to $30 for a weekly trip to a decent restaurant.

"I was so surprised my freshman year at how much money I blew through the first semester," says Kim Powers (Ithaca College, Class of 2005). "There were certain nights I couldn't go out and do things because I simply did not have the money." Food was one of the top expenses, she realized. She and her friends frequently partook in a college tradition—ordering in late at night—and the costs added up faster than a pepperoni pie disappears during finals week.

Cutting down on those expenses is not easy, but it's not impossible, either. It usually comes down to a combination of self-discipline and the ability to maximize the cash that you do have.

"College students get very creative when it comes to having a limited cash flow," says Sabryna Phillips of Loyola Marymount University. When it comes to food, for example, she suggests keeping an eye out for the many campus events where snacks are there for the taking.

For the times that you get pizza or fast food, keep an eye out for coupons or specials. Even if you only get a free soda out of the deal, that's still an extra dollar or two in your pocket.

When it comes to her budget, Amelia Hall always takes care of essentials first, and considers any other expenses, such as dining out, to be luxuries. She avoids going out to eat, and tries to save extra money from her part-time job for crises that inevitably arise.

No matter what size town or city your college is located in, there are bound to be a number of free or low-cost entertainment options. University of Pennsylvania student Darryl B. Wooten has taken advantage of cultural offerings at his school and in the city of Philadelphia. Find those events, he advises, by reading guides and newspapers, and inquiring at information kiosks on campus and in the city.

He's learned that some city art galleries serve free refreshments on Fridays—making it a great campus escape, combining culture and food for little to no money. Darryl suggests going with a group of friends: "This is terrific way to bond with your classmates, do fun and exciting things, and save money in the process."

> *"Going to school in a major city, I have found that it is very easy to spend a lot of money in a short period of time, but also very possible to entertain yourself for little to nothing at all. All it requires is a little research and creativity."*
>
> —Darryl B. Wooten, University of Pennsylvania, Class of 2005

Northwestern University student Jake Carter lives in an off-campus apartment and agrees that getting friends involved can keep a lid on expenses. Instead of going out to dinner, a group of students can plan a meal, for example, with one or two taking charge each time. Making the meal together can be more fun than going out to eat. And the costs won't be too high if students plan sensibly. "Almost all college students are in the same boat financially, so it helps if you split costs among a group of people," says Jake.

On a personal level, Jake follows a sensible financial plan that's guaranteed to work: He sets a budget and sticks to it, with fixed expenses—rent, utilities, water, and parking—in one section that can't be tapped for other reasons. "I've found that I tend to spend a lot of my money on food, especially eating out with friends," he says. "But having a budget helps me to gauge how often I can do so without getting in trouble."

Keeping Your Expenses in Check

Students say that by employing these strategies—many of which are related to food costs—they've been able to stretch their dollars:

- ❑ **Don't be so quick to skip the dining hall.** "I have a meal plan on campus, so I rarely go out to eat during the times I have a prepaid meal waiting for me in the servery," says Becky Thilo. It may not be fine dining, but with some creativity, you can usually have a decent meal. The company's pretty good, too. Where it's permitted, take a cookie or piece of fruit to eat later, instead of heading to a vending machine or a snack bar.
- ❑ **Get a dining hall meal-to-go if necessary.** Most colleges with meal plans offer this option for students who are unable to get to the dining hall during lunch hours, perhaps due to a job or off-campus committment. This can easily save you the $5 or more you'd spend at a pizzeria or burger joint.
- ❑ **Realize that in order to save money, you'll have to deny yourself some things.** Sometimes, there are no shortcuts, and the only way to afford a Saturday night out is to stay in on Friday. Of course, that doesn't mean you have to spend the night reading or watching TV. "On our campus, every weekend there are numerous things going on campus for free or really cheap," says Kim Powers of Ithaca College. "There are musical performances, campus-wide programs, and movies playing in our lecture halls for only $2. You are getting out of your room, but at the same time, saving money."
- ❑ **Limit trips to restaurants.** Becky Thilo, for example, will only dine out on Saturday nights—when Rice University's dining halls are closed. Next time you're desperate for a break from cafeteria meals and want something more than fast food consider less-expensive alternatives to full-service restaurants. A gourmet precooked meal at a supermarket (take it home to heat it up) might cost $10, which is much less than you'd pay at a restaurant, especially after the tip and drinks are included.
- ❑ **Shop around, and take advantage of sales.** From textbooks to clothes, know where you can get the best buys and do your shopping in those places.

continued

Keeping Your Expenses in Check (continued)

- ❑ **Get a job.** Even working just five hours a week can give you the spending money to enjoy your free time a little more. Keep in mind that when you're working, you're not spending money, either.
- ❑ **Take advantage of free or low-cost cultural offerings in your college's home city.** "You can get into many movies, museums, art galleries, concerts, plays, and much more for discounted prices if you bring your student ID," says Darryl B. Wooten, of the University of Pennsylvania. "These places thrive on the business brought in by college students, so they are very willing to offer deals to those who are proactive enough to inquire about them."
- ❑ **Consider moving off campus.** Although many colleges require students to live in campus housing for at least one year, off-campus living might be a cheaper choice, especially if you have one or more roommates. And depending on your eating habits, you might end up spending less compared to the cost of your on-campus meal plan.

Should I apply to be an R.A.?

One of the most appealing jobs on campus—at least as the benefits go—might be the position of Resident Adviser or Resident Assistant, also known as an R.A. Although compensation packages vary from school to school, most R.A.s receive free room and board, plus compensation for telephone charges and similar expenses. For students facing student-loan debt and for their parents, who are paying $25,000 or much more for tuition at some schools, it can seem like a natural choice, since room and board alone can cost $5,000 to $10,000 a year.

Many of the students interviewed in this book have served as Resident Advisers, and their helpful nature shows. They overwhelmingly have positive things to say about being an R.A., but they also point out that it requires a good deal of sacrifice.

"I've worked in the position, and the rewards are far greater than you can imagine," says Codie Thurston (University of Alaska

Anchorage, Class of 2006). "But I do caution that the responsibilities are greater than you initially consider as well. You will be put in situations with your peers that require you to enforce the rules, rather than break them. Often this creates conflicts in personal relationships."

But when students like Codie talk about the rewards of being an R.A., money isn't on their minds—rather, it's the benefits they get from being part of a leadership team, from helping students find their way, and from making a difference on campus. In short, they embrace their responsibilities because they know how the position benefits their personal growth; the free room and board are an added bonus.

Adam Lucido, for example, says he never refers to his Resident Adviser position as a job. Instead, he views it as an opportunity to get to know more people on campus and to make that campus a better place. He calls his role in building a strong community on his dorm's floor "the most rewarding experience" and a "total blast" to do.

"If working with people and taking time from yourself for others is something that you love doing, then go for it [applying to be an R.A.]. If you'd rather go off, do homework, and party, then you'll just be unhappy as an R.A."

—David Thompson, Lehigh University, Class of 2006

Another consideration several students pointed out: If you are thinking of applying to be an R.A. for the financial benefits, ask what it might do to your current financial aid package. Joseph Vera (Northwestern University, Class of 2007), for example, learned that his financial aid would drop because the R.A. compensation would be viewed as a form of financial assistance. "Before you start applying to become an R.A., sit down with a financial aid adviser and talk over your package," says Joseph.

To get an idea whether the position is right for you, take a look at your own R.A. and consider how she balances the position's demands with her academics and personal life. Could you balance everything? Could you handle the responsibilities? Are you prepared to not live with your friends, but rather with mostly freshmen and sophomores whom you don't know?

Talk to your R.A., or hall director, and see what opportunities are possible at your school. But no matter what you do, pursue the position only if you could do the job well, recommends David Thompson. "I know R.A.s who do the job and get full financial benefits and hate it, where there are others like me who enjoy it, yet because of financial aid don't see nearly the same financial benefit from it."

How can I find a job that will complement my studies?

Wherever you earn your college cash, you'll have to strike a balance between your work and your studies. One of the best ways to do this is to find a job that in some way connects to your field of study.

For example, with a dual major in political science and secondary education, Chris Diem (Texas A & M University, Class of 2005) wanted to gain experience in both fields. But he also wanted to earn some spending money. Chris got a job as a substitute teacher during breaks from school, when he was home in Harker Heights, Texas. And he spent the summer before his senior year knocking on doors for a congressional candidate. Both were paid positions. "Both are at the bottom level, but both are great entry ways to future jobs," he says.

Where to begin your search? One place to start, students say, is to apply a point emphasized earlier in this book: Get to know your professors. "A friend of mine is a biology major and loves spending time in the lab," says Becky Thilo. The friend simply asked one of her professors about her research projects—and inquired if she needed any help. The move has paid off handsomely: "Not only has my friend established a great relationship with her professor, but she also makes money doing work specific to her major."

Other good opportunities, Becky points out, include work as an undergraduate teaching assistant, grader, or a tutor—positions that at least require an applicant to have excelled in the course as a student. Not all schools offer all positions, and the compensation can range from a minimal stipend to a regular paycheck to tuition reimbursement. To find out how it works, you'll have to ask around—which itself can help open doors. "Contacting the professor and establishing a relationship will always give you a leg up on the competition," Becky adds.

If your professors or the department hosting your major do not have openings for help, don't forget a helpful follow-up question: "Can you suggest anywhere else I should check?" The answer might reveal a lead that's worth checking out. "If the departments are not hiring, they can generally give you an idea of where to look for good opportunities and which people or companies are most interested in hiring students under a specific field of study," says Darryl B. Wooten. He also advises talking to upperclassmen to see how they found jobs to complement their studies.

In addition to getting to know faculty members, another good way to get involved in your major—and open up possible job opportunities—is to be active in student organizations related to your field of study, suggests Amelia Hall. Recruiters often appeal directly to these organizations because they know that the membership is filled with students who are passionate about the field.

You probably won't join an organization just in hopes of getting a job, though. Think about the bigger picture, and the more likely chain of events: Your interest in the field will grow. You'll hear about the experiences of people in the field. You'll develop your own curiosities—and you'll be better prepared to act on them. Such students, by nature, are more likely to find a job that's a good fit.

That approach worked for Chelsea Church (Michigan State University, Class of 2006), who found a paid internship at a public relations firm as a result of her involvement in her school's chapter of the Public Relations Student Society of America. "We are told to 'network, network, network' and this group allows me to do so," says Chelsea. A past president of the group and another friend alerted her to the internship opportunity because they had previously worked for the firm; her friend even put in a good word for her.

While students shouldn't feel they absolutely need connections to get ahead, the reality is that they help. A strong recommendation from someone with experience in the field (especially within the firm you're applying to) carries weight. Put yourself in the shoes of the person doing the hiring, and you'll see why. And the only way to get those recommendations—and tips about available job openings—is to circulate and get involved in your field. "Meet people . . . the more you network, the more apt you are to find a career-related job," Chelsea says.

Becca Hatton landed both of her paid internships through the internship coordinator at West Virginia University's Perley Isaac Reed School of Journalism. One was a summer position with an international public relations firm, while the other was with the university's News and Information Services division. "If you go to them, they will help you as best they can," says Becca of the internship coordinator. "As long as you work hard and show that you can do more than the average person, you can do anything you want." Becca also credits WVU alumni connections with helping her secure the summer job.

To get involved in your field, Amelia Hall suggests checking out every opportunity: going to the campus employment office, checking out campus bulletin boards, and attending job fairs that are usually staged at the beginning of the year. "Fill out lots of applications for jobs you're interested in—don't bet everything on one application," she says.

Lastly, not everyone will be fortunate enough to get a part-time job directly related to their major. Just keep in mind that a job can connect to your career objectives in less-than-obvious ways. For example, dining hall work—a job not usually revered on college campuses—can lead to promotions for those who take their duties seriously. Any employer in any field can appreciate the leadership qualities demonstrated by a "student manager" or someone who has earned a similar title. It means you are responsible, well-organized, and dependable. And it's far, far, better than having no work experience at all.

Index